Bob Prentiss has it right when [...] *ourselves.* **iMOTIVATEme** *reveals new* [...] *format that will make your self-motivation stick. By the end, you will honestly be able to say... "I motivate me!"*
  — Vicki Hess, Employee Engagement Expert and
  Author of *SHIFT to Professional Paradise*

When you work your way through **iMOTIVATEme**, *your vision for your life becomes your reality.*
  — Judith Barrett, Executive Director, Ability 1st

Motivational speakers meet a need... sometimes we need a verbal boot-in-the-pants to get going. But it's self-motivation that keeps us moving and makes us successful. Bob Prentiss shows us how to motivate ourselves. His model is well researched and simple, and most importantly, it works!
  — Dan Clark, Author, Speaker, Consultant, Coach

Motivation is the fuel for the engine that moves us to the place we want to be in our lives. In **iMOTIVATEme**, *Bob Prentiss serves up "high octane" fuel for reaching your goals and objectives. He provides readers with both the concepts and immediate action plans to make significant changes and accomplish significant goals in their work, family, civic and other important aspects of their lives.*
  — Roy Reid, APR, CPRC, Author of *Outrageous Trust*® and
  Partner, Consensus Communications

Bob Prentiss's inspired motivational approach is a godsend for those who are frustrated by their lack of success in achieving personal goals. It taps into the visionary in each of us and allows for the "successability" of everyone by providing deeply researched and insightfully pragmatic tools for becoming the person each one of us would like to be.
  — Rev. Richard W. Jobe, Founder of Random Access Music
  and Adjunct Professor at Martin Methodist College

iMOTIVATEme *is a terrific combination of concept, process and practicality. It places responsibility for achieving goals gently yet firmly where it belongs — with the individual — and provides each of us with a logical process for success.*

    – Al Lucia, President, ADL Associates, Inc.

In **iMOTIVATEme**, *Bob Prentiss has found fresh ways to present both enduring perspectives about motivation and practical new tools for increasing it.* **iMOTIVATEme** *includes an array of exercises designed with options that allow the reader to tailor a personalized step-by-step approach to making needed changes. The book is well-paced and practical, but also provides a theoretical overview that ties things together for the reader who wants to know the "whys" as well as the "hows."*

    – Kenneth W. Christian, Ph.D., Licensed Psychologist and Author of *Your Own Worst Enemy: Breaking the Habit of Adult Underachievement*

iMOTIVATEme *presents a systematic and detailed approach to understanding and improving one's personal motivation. As important as that is, Bob's underlying motivation is to help us help ourselves faster, better, smarter and more consistently. Motivation is an inside job…and now we all have the job description!*

    – Kevin W. McCarthy, Author of *The On-Purpose Person*

iMOTIVATEme *offers a realistic, how-to approach for achieving your goals through self-motivation.*

    – Judy B. Barnes, Counseling Specialist, Tallahassee Community College

iMotivate
me

Take Control of Your Motivation to Reach Your Goals and Achieve Your Dreams

5/23/2012

Milt,
Best Wishes

Bob

P.S. Thanks for taking me to the Governor's Club for my going away event!

Bob Prentiss, JD, MS, DTM

iMotivate *me*

Take Control of Your Motivation to Reach Your Goals and Achieve Your Dreams

Copyright © 2012 Bob A. Prentiss. All rights reserved.

Cover image copyright © iStockPhoto.com.

No part of this book may be reproduced in any form without written permission in advance from the publisher. International rights and foreign translations available only through negotiation with Tiger Arts Communications.

Inquiries regarding permission for use of the material contained in this book should be addressed to:
Tiger Arts Communications
P.O. Box 6676
Tallahassee, FL 32314
850-284-0233

Printed in the United States of America
ISBN: 978-0-615-31010-7

Credits
Collaborative Editor   Juli Baldwin, The Baldwin Group, Dallas, TX
                              Juli@BaldwinGrp.com
Copy Editor   Kathleen Green, Positively Proofed, Plano, TX
                              info@PositivelyProofed.com
Design, art direction, and production   Melissa Monogue, Back Porch Creative, Plano, TX
                              info@BackPorchCreative.com

Motivate a man, and he is on task for a day; teach him how to motivate himself, and he is on task for a lifetime.

Acknowledgements

No man is an island, and no author stands alone. This book would not exist were it not for the assistance of several people. The first are my professors at Florida State University where I received my Master's in Instructional Design and became fascinated with the subject of motivation. Special thanks go to Mary Kate McKee. Without her continuous assistance, I would never have completed my degree. I'm sure I'm not the only student who feels this way about Mary Kate.

I would also like to acknowledge the help of friends Mohammad Sherif, Ellie Simon and Tricia Elton.

Thanks to my Toastmaster friends, especially Elaine Thornburg, Wayne and Margaret Warren, and Dan Clark, for all they have done and continue to do in furthering my development as a speaker.

And lastly, thanks to Wendy Kurtz of Elizabeth Charles & Associates, LLC for her guidance and for helping me find editor Juli Baldwin, of The Baldwin Group, and graphic designer, Melissa Monogue of Back Porch Creative.

CONTENTS

Introduction ... i

How to Use This Book to Create
   Your Own Motivation Plan ... vii

Part I – The VSE™ Model for Self-Motivation ... 1
1. Why Motivate Yourself? ... 3
2. Vision ... 13
3. Successability ... 29
4. Successability: Divide & Conquer ... 43
5. Environment ... 63

Part II – Strategies to Increase Your Motivation ... 77
6. Detractors ... 79
7. Enhancers ... 101

Part III – Putting It All Together ... 115
8. Create Your Unique Motivation Plan ... 117
9. Continuous Improvement ... 129

Take Charge of Your Motivation ... 141

Bonus Section: Sample Self-Motivation Plans ... 145
✦ Health and Fitness ... 145
✦ Career/Job Change ... 154
✦ Finances ... 162

Index ... 173

About the Author ... 175

Introduction

Do you have a dream that always seems just out of reach?

Is there something about your life that you want to change? Maybe it involves a career change like a better paying, more stimulating job. Or perhaps a change that will improve your personal life, such as a healthier lifestyle or a more loving, caring relationship.

Do you keep making the decision to change – *this time, for real* – to buckle down and get it done, only to find yourself once again waylaid, off course and maybe even a little bit depressed? Perhaps you know you have the talent and ability to accomplish your goal, but for some reason you can't "stick with it" long enough to achieve it.

Is starting a project easy, but finishing difficult? Do you wonder why everything seems to distract you and you can't stay on track? Are you frustrated and annoyed with yourself and possibly thinking less of yourself for not having it together?

Have you read motivational books or listened to motivational speakers and been pumped … for awhile … and then lost your motivation?

Join the crowd. You're not alone.

"Sticking to it" is a challenge most of us face at some point in our lives. And … it's not your fault. There's not something lacking in your character that makes you unable to finish a project or achieve your goals. In fact, I'm quite certain that you are fully capable of achieving anything you desire to accomplish.

If there is a change you want to make in your life that you haven't been able to make a reality, odds are it's because you aren't motivated. The initial excitement of a new project or big goal is enough to get you motivated and sustain you for a while. But once that initial excitement wears off – especially if you hit a bump in the road or another exciting project or goal starts to distract you – suddenly your motivation evaporates.

I believe a lot of people are just like me. We were good students and are productive employees because we work within someone else's structure. When we went to school, teachers played a big role in our motivation. And typically, our boss or manager, top leadership and the company culture all impact our motivation at work. We are motivated by someone or something such as a paycheck, the satisfaction of a job well done, fear of getting fired, an academic grading system or peer pressure.

But outside of structure, we tend to have a difficult time staying motivated. When it comes to working on our own projects or achieving our own goals – like starting a business, writing a book, getting fit or finishing a degree – we can't seem to make it happen. Why? Because there isn't a teacher or manager to make sure we stay on task. And most of us don't have the money or the means to have a motivational coach by our side 24 hours a day, seven days a week, to keep us motivated.

***Self-motivation* is the solution.**

And that is a good thing, because motivation is highly personal. No teacher, manager or coach will ever know you as well as you know yourself. The problem is that very few of us have been taught how to motivate ourselves. We're taught how to dream and to set goals by our families and friends, self-help gurus and even TV. But no

Introduction

one ever teaches us how to motivate ourselves so we can start moving toward and *keep* moving toward our goals and dreams.

I've been that non-motivated person who can't seem to make it happen. As long as I can remember, I've wanted to be a public speaker ... to stand in front of admiring crowds who hang on my every word. I remember watching Robert Kennedy speak. I'd close my eyes and see myself, cool and competent, dressed in a tailor-cut navy blue suit, the audience in the palm of my hand. I had a dream.

But for the longest time, the dream had not become reality. Instead of pursuing my passion, I got my bachelor's degree and went to law school. I studied hard, got good grades and got a job sitting at a desk, reading law books and drafting documents. It was a pleasant job that paid a decent wage, and I worked for nice people who appreciated my work. But it wasn't my dream, and I felt no passion.

Occasionally I'd take baby steps toward my dream, but I didn't follow up on those baby steps. And since I already had a job, I had to work on my public speaking after hours, and I just couldn't get motivated to do that. It was upsetting. I was frustrated with my inability to achieve my dream or to even take consistent steps toward achieving it. The vision I had of myself was so different than the reality of my existence. I had an image of who I knew I *could* be, yet I knew I wasn't that person. Because of that conflict, I set out to discover why my wonderful *what could be* was not my *what was*.

Luckily (if you believe in luck) I just happened to be working on my master's degree in education and was studying the role of motivation in learning. I realized that even though I *wanted* to become a professional speaker, I wasn't *motivated* to become one. I also realized that in order to succeed, not only would I have to *become* motivated, I'd have to stay motivated. From those first insights sprang the most important realization: *I was going to have to motivate myself.* No one else could do it for me. So I decided to learn all I could about motivation, particularly self-motivation, and then I made it my mission to share what I'd learned.

There is an old adage, attributed to many different sources, that says: "Give a man a fish, you feed him for a day; teach him how to fish, you feed him for his life." I've adapted that to: **Motivate a man, and he is on task for a day; teach him how to motivate himself, and he is on task for a lifetime.**

That is my objective in writing this book – to teach you how to motivate yourself. I am not a "motivational" author or speaker. In fact, I like to think of myself as The Non-Motivational Speaker™, because I can't motivate you to do anything – only you can do that. Instead, I am a teacher – a teacher of self-motivation. And once you learn how to motivate yourself, you can do it without my help.

iMOTIVATEme presents a proven model for self-motivation based on studies by researchers at major universities in the fields of educational motivation, sports motivation and employment motivation. Rather than a series of behaviors designed to motivate the "average" person, my self-motivation model recognizes that we are all unique. What motivates me is not what motivates you. This is what makes the self-motivation model different and much more effective. The model offers a practical way for you to determine what motivates you – and what doesn't – and then guides you step by step through the process of **creating your own motivation plan, tailor made *for* you, *by* you**. With a customized plan, you are guaranteed to not only become motivated, but also to stay motivated.

Life today is more stressful than ever. It takes all of our energy just to get through the day and handle our responsibilities at work and

Introduction

at home. For most of us, that usually means we have nothing left when it comes time to work on those things that are truly important to us. As author Billy Cox says, "If your dreams and goals are getting the 'leftovers' of your life, you'll never achieve them."

Time doesn't stop running just because we don't use it well. If you are going to achieve the change you want in your life, you're going to have to take responsibility for your motivation. If you don't, another year will go by … and then another … and another. And you'll still be in the same place, doing the same thing, wishing things were better … just like I was.

Self-motivation is the piece you've been missing. I know firsthand that learning how to motivate yourself will make all the difference. When you can motivate yourself, you will be able to:

- Stay focused on your objective;
- Stick with your plans and consistently take action;
- Ignore those oh-so-interesting distractions;
- Minimize your disappointment and frustration during challenges and rough times;
- Make your goals and dreams a reality.

In short, you will discover that your life really can be exciting and fulfilling.

It is my sincere hope that you will apply the information in this book to achieve whatever it is in life you want to accomplish – big or small, personal or professional. I know you can do it.

Bob Prentiss

iMotivate*me*

How to Use This Book to Create Your Own Motivation Plan

The fundamental principle underlying the concept of self-motivation is that you are in charge. This is good news, but it's also bad news. The good news is that you have total responsibility for your motivation. The bad news is that you have total responsibility for your motivation. When it comes to your motivation, there's no one else for you to rely on.

So how do you carry out this important assignment, being in charge of your motivation?

In order to become and stay motivated, we must become intentional men and women. My intention in writing this book is that with it you will learn how to motivate yourself. To do this, however, requires more of you than just reading. Though you may indeed learn some of the concepts by simply reading them, to apply them to your life will require active participation. You will need to spend time reflecting on and learning who you are, your likes and dislikes, the things that motivate you and the things that de-motivate you.

To facilitate this self-awareness, I've included some thought-starter questions throughout the book. (You will recognize these by their title, "**MOTIVATE***me*.") I strongly urge you to complete them, as they will help you not only understand the material, but also integrate the strategies into your daily life. I recommend that you answer these questions as you encounter them in the book, rather than reading the book all the way through and then completing them. You will also find free tools and resources on my website: **www.iMotivateMeTheBook.com**.

Throughout this book, I will share many strategies that will help you increase your motivation. But not every strategy will work for every person. Try the ones that resonate with you and that you think will positively impact your motivation and keep you on task. Consider how you can modify the strategies, or fine-tune them, so that they become even more powerful. These customized strategies will turbo-boost your motivation.

But even with solid concepts and strategies, you cannot count on motivation just happening. The old saw, "If you fail to plan, you plan to fail," is nowhere more true than in motivating yourself. Consequently, a key aspect of self-motivation is to develop a customized plan. As you read and answer the questions, you will begin to create this plan. At the end of the book, you will put your motivation plan in writing using a Motivation Map. This is where it will all come together. Your Motivation Map will be a visual representation of your unique plan for self-motivation – a tangible object you can use daily to show you exactly what you need to do to manifest the change you want in your life.

If there is one lesson I've learned over the years, it's that what I get out of any endeavor is directly proportional to what I put into it. This will certainly be the case for you with this book. Use it like the resource it is. Answer the thought-starter questions, be your own boss and give yourself the assignment to make a motivation plan and to write it down. It might take a little more effort and work to design a customized motivation plan than to read a series of generic tips and hints, but your dreams and goals are worth it.

Part I

THE VSE™ MODEL
FOR SELF-MOTIVATION

iMotivateme

one

Why Motivate Yourself?

*Motivation is a fire from within.
If someone else tries to light that fire under you,
chances are it will burn very briefly.*
STEPHEN COVEY

You may wonder why you need to motivate yourself. Aren't there some great motivational books and speakers out there? Sure there are! The speaker I heard most recently was Zig Ziglar. Anyone who has heard him knows he's a very accomplished speaker. I walked out of his talk totally motivated. I was ready to move the world ... to kick butt and take names!

But then one week later, there I was, doing what I do best – sitting in front of the TV, remote in hand, vegging out. My dream was to become a public speaker. But after a long day at the office, all I wanted to do was pop a dinner into the microwave, open a cold one, and sit myself down in front of a good action movie.

The problem I faced – and so many of us face – is twofold. First, Zig Ziglar is not available to me when I most need his help. Wouldn't it be great to have Zig with me 24/7, encouraging me when I'm at my weakest? I suppose I could listen to one of his audios or read one of his books ... *if* I have enough motivation to struggle against my inertia to do it.

But there's an important reason why a motivational audio or book isn't going to be very effective. It's the same reason why motivational speakers aren't all that helpful *in the long run*. The reason is that motivational speakers and authors present generic information, designed for the "average person" ... whomever that is. I'm not suggesting that these resources don't have good information; most do. My concern is that they don't constitute a program for becoming and *remaining* motivated. Nor do they take into account that each of us is different – and that is the second part of the problem.

Each of us has different likes and dislikes. I like action movies; you like comedy or horror. I like salty treats; you like sweet treats. What motivates each of us is different, too. What motivates you may not be what motivates me and vice versa. I may be motivated by promising myself some kind of reward if I complete a task or project. You, however, may be motivated by the feeling of satisfaction you get when you cross tasks off your to-do list. Similarly, what drains me of my motivation may not be what zaps yours. I absolutely freeze in my path (lose my motivation) when faced with a task I don't know how to do. You, on the other hand, may love the challenge of such a task and tear into it.

Motivational talks, books and audios are generic, not customized for any one of us. Consequently, they are not *optimized* for any one of us. They simply cannot provide the motivational power we can provide for ourselves when we create our own motivation plan.

The only way to get around these two problems – Zig Ziglar not being with us 24/7 and each of us having a unique motivational character – is to be in charge of our own motivation. In other words, the solution is self-motivation.

Each of us must become our own motivator so that we can be there 24/7 when we most need motivation – after the kids have gone to bed and we're faced with two choices: Do we have a glass of wine and watch TV, or do we work on our project/goal? And when we take responsibility for our motivation, we can create a plan that is uniquely ours, rather than a generic message aimed at the masses.

What is Motivation?

The first step in learning how to get and stay motivated is to answer the question, "What is motivation?"

According to Harold Koontz and Cyril O'Donnell, "To motivate is to induce people to act in a certain way." In K.P. Sharma's book *Entrepreneurship*, W.G. Scott gives this definition: "Motivation means a process of stimulating people to action to accomplish desired goals." And Dr. John Keller, professor at Florida State University, describes motivation this way: "Ability is what a person *can* do. Motivation is what a person *will* do." Basically, he's telling us that the difference between merely wishing for our goals and dreams and actually achieving them is motivation.

> **Motivation**
> A force that compels us to take action toward a specific goal.

When I think of motivation, I see an image of a locomotive in front of a string of railroad cars. The locomotive is the power that moves the cars. Without the locomotive, the cars don't move. Likewise, without motivation, you and I don't move; we just sit still and accomplish nothing. My definition of motivation is: **a force that compels us to take action toward a specific goal.**

Now that we understand what motivation is, perhaps the next question is, "How do people become motivated?"

Motivational Models

When I was working on my Master's in Education in Instructional Design, I became fascinated with the idea that I needed to build motivation into my designs. So I began studying the various theories and models of motivation, first in education and then in athletics and the workplace.

I found that the most comprehensive motivation models had some common elements:

1. There must be something important the person wants to achieve.
2. The person must feel that he is capable of achieving what he wants.
3. The person's environment significantly impacts motivation.

I also noticed something interesting about the existing models and definitions: They are all outwardly focused – one person motivating another. In education, the models are about teachers motivating learners. In athletics, it's coaches motivating athletes. And in the workplace, it is managers and leaders motivating their workers.

But I was searching for a model that would show a person how to motivate him/herself. I wanted a model that would allow each of us to design a customized, optimized plan that we could apply to ourselves, 24 hours a day, seven days a week, even on holidays if we wanted. Not finding such a model, I decided to develop my own.

The VSE™ Model for Self-Motivation

To create my model, I took this wealth of information about how to motivate other people and turned it 180 degrees and adapted it to a person who wants to motivate himself. My model is based on the idea that self-motivation is influenced by three factors: the *Vision*, something I call *Successability*, and *Environment*.

The model is best described as a mathematical function (think back to high school math):

SELF-MOTIVATION = f (VISION, SUCCESSABILITY, ENVIRONMENT)

This is the VSE™ Model for Self-Motivation. (I pronounce it "vizzy.") At first glance, the model may appear complicated, but actually it is easy to understand. Just as important, it's a practical way to stay motivated (*practical* meaning it's easy to put into practice). Basically, the model states that self-motivation is a function of three factors:

1. **Vision** – a change you want to make in your life; a project or dream you want to accomplish;
2. **Successability** – your confidence in your ability to achieve the Vision; your belief and expectancy that you can attain it;
3. **Environment** – your physical environment (the place where you work on your Vision) and your social environment (the people, support systems and experiences with which you surround yourself).

Any change – positive or negative – in any of the three factors causes a corresponding change in motivation. Make your Vision more desirable, and your motivation will increase. Take action to increase your Successability, your motivation will increase. Surround yourself with people who support you (Environment), your motivation will increase. This relationship among the factors is best illustrated by a visual representation of the model:

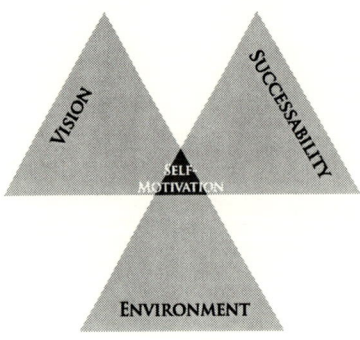 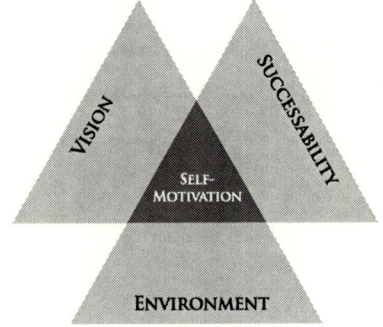

The VSE Model of Self-Motivation   Increase any of the three factors to increase self-motivation

Think about a time in your life when you were extremely motivated to accomplish something, then consider what made you so motivated. Chances are, you had a strong desire to achieve your goal, you were reasonably confident that you could achieve it, and your circumstances and the people around you supported your efforts. That was the VSE model in action.

But the model is even more powerful because the three factors of self-motivation are not independent of one another; instead they are *interrelated*. That means that improving one factor will not only positively impact your motivation, but also will often positively impact another factor, which in turn will positively impact your motivation even more. Consequently, **improving any of the three factors increases your motivation exponentially**.

For example, people who have high levels of confidence in themselves (Successability) are more likely to use the resources available in their Social Environment. They will seek out relationships that will help them achieve their goals. As a result, their confidence and motivation will increase even more. Those who feel less confident, on the other hand, are less likely to pursue these relationships, so they will lack the support and other benefits such relationships can provide. As a result, their confidence in their ability to achieve their goal will diminish even more, as will their motivation.

The implication of this interrelatedness is that you need to work on all three factors. Focusing on all three factors gives you three times as many opportunities to increase your motivation. And because the three are interrelated, the outcome will usually be more than three times as much motivation. The rest of this book is dedicated to teaching you strategies that will positively influence each of the three factors so that you can maximize your motivation.

Motivating yourself is a science with rules. The science is the self-motivation model. Learn the rules of self-motivation, apply them to your situation and you will achieve your dreams.

Intention is the Key to Motivation

Perhaps the best part of the VSE model is that you have complete control over the three factors and, therefore, complete control over your motivation. We exercise control over our motivation by acting intentionally rather than acting automatically.

Viktor Fankl was a Nazi concentration camp survivor. After he was liberated, he wrote a book, *Man's Search for Meaning*, about his time in the camp. In the book, he points out the difference between man and other animals. Animals act only on instinct – a stimulus triggers an automatic reaction. Instinct works very well in the animal kingdom. In fact, it's crucial to survival. A zebra smells a lion (stimulus) and immediately runs (action). There's no debating, no figuring out the odds that the lion will eat another zebra. The zebra just runs automatically.

Instinct: stimulus ⟹ action

Humans act on instinct, as well. Like the zebra, we instinctively run from danger. But we also have the power to choose our responses. Frankl differentiates us from animals in this unique ability to receive a stimulus and decide how we want to respond. He calls this ability *reflection*. Of course, just because we have this ability doesn't mean we always use it. When we react without reflection, we operate automatically. Our life is then shaped by external forces – perhaps another person, a situation or our history. When this happens, we often say someone or something is "pushing our buttons."

Automatic: stimulus ⟹ action

Reflection occurs in the space between stimulus and action. This middle step is where we have the power to *choose* the action we take. By being aware of that middle ground, and our ability to operate in that special place, we can become intentional about our actions rather than simply reacting.

Intentional: stimulus ⟹ reflection ⟹ action

When we act with intention, we are not pulled off-course by distractions, we stay focused on the task at hand, and we process information without being unduly influenced by our emotions. Think for a moment about times in your life when you acted automatically and times when you acted with intention. Would you say you more often act automatically or intentionally?

Acting with intention allows us to be *conscious* in our choices, meaning we can consciously choose to positively affect the three factors in the VSE model. Furthermore, any step we take with intent exercises our control, which research shows is inherently motivating. I experienced this firsthand when I tried my hand at writing a screenplay for a romantic comedy. As I was writing it, I was extremely motivated because I was in total control of the process. I worked on it at least three evenings a week. But once it was completed, I had to find someone to buy it. That was difficult. People either rejected it outright or just didn't bother to respond. I had little control over what these other people did, so I struggled to stay motivated to market it.

Trying to sell my screenplay has taught me the importance of self-motivation because, ultimately, **achieving a goal or dream is dependent on what *you* do rather than what others do** (or don't do).

It may seem a bit ironic, but one of the best ways to guarantee you act intentionally is by developing good habits. This was brought home to me one day when I was talking with a friend who is constantly fighting his weight. He's tried several different weight-loss plans. One thing I notice about these diets is that they generally require you to keep a log of the food you eat. Everything that goes into your mouth gets written down. The act of logging your food makes you conscious of what you're eating and, therefore, more intentional about your choices. With my friend, it seems the first thing to go in the diet plan is the log. Once that goes, it becomes much easier for him to slip into being an unconscious and automatic eater.

The same concept holds true with motivation. The more intentional you are, the more successful you will be at motivating yourself and, consequently, achieving the change you want in your life. A habit I developed to ensure that I remain intentional is keeping my weekly to-do list on the top of my desk. As soon as I sit down at my desk, I immediately check the list for the actions I need to take that week. As you study the strategies in this book, decide which ones will work best for you and think about how you could make them into habits.

As for my screenplay, I'm still looking for a buyer. Has my motivation suffered? Yes, at times. Will your motivation suffer as you pursue your dreams? Yes. The simple truth is there will be times when you're not motivated – it's just part of being human. And that's precisely why self-motivation is so important. When you find that you've lost your motivation to achieve change in your life, you will now be able to take control, act with intention and re-motivate yourself. You won't have to rely on anyone or anything else for your motivation.

SUMMARY

- ❖ You are responsible for motivating yourself; no one else will do it for you.

- ❖ Self-motivation is influenced by three factors:
    - ✦ Vision – what you want to accomplish
    - ✦ Successability – your confidence in your ability to achieve it
    - ✦ Environment – your physical and social surroundings

- ❖ Modifying or varying any of the three factors will impact – positively or negatively – your motivation.

- ❖ Motivating yourself is a science with rules. Learn the rules of self-motivation and apply them to your situation, and you will achieve your dreams.

- ❖ Acting with intention is crucial to positively impacting the three factors of self-motivation.

two

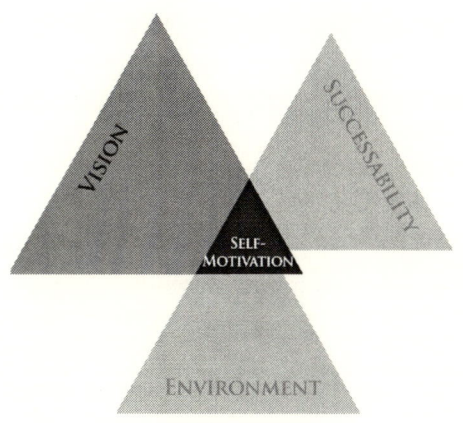

Vision

You can achieve any change you might desire in your life by learning how to motivate yourself. Throughout the next several chapters, you will begin to use your intention to increase your motivation by focusing on the individual factors of the Self-Motivation Model, starting with the Vision.

More than likely, you were drawn to this book because there is something you want to accomplish or change in your life, but you've been stymied in your efforts to make it happen. That dream or change you seek is the Vision.

The Vision can be a desired change in any area of your life. It might involve your career or perhaps relate to your finances, health and fitness, or even recreation and fun. It can include, for example, your manner of living, relationships you wish to develop, skills you would like to master, knowledge or self-understanding you want to cultivate, or travel and adventure you'd like to pursue. The Vision can be an all-encompassing idea, such as understanding your purpose in life or why you are on the planet. But it also can be much more narrow or specific, like finding a new job, writing a book or learning photography.

The Vision gives us a destination and a focus for our motivation. The Vision is crucial, because until we know where we are going, we will have no idea how to get there. Without a Vision, we will be unfocused and unmotivated.

There are two key aspects of the Vision:
    1. It must be worthwhile.
    2. It must be clear.

Let's look at each of these in depth.

Make the Vision Worthwhile

If the Vision is going to motivate you, it must be worthwhile to you. This is really two different requirements: 1) worthwhile, and 2) to you.

> **Vision**
> A worthwhile pursuit;
> an important change you want to make in your life.

First, the Vision must be a *worthy* pursuit. Virtually every theory of motivation concurs that if the change you're trying to make is not relevant, valuable and applicable to your life, you likely will not be motivated to take the steps necessary to achieve it. Case in point: I used to dream of traveling to South America and speaking Spanish with the locals. Note that my dream was not to learn how to speak Spanish or to practice it regularly. But to manifest such a Vision, I would have to do both. Ultimately, I decided the dream simply wasn't worthy enough to put forth the required effort to bring it to fruition.

A friend of mine had a dream to become a physician's assistant who works with children. To do this, she needed an advanced degree that would require her to go back to school for several years. The question she had to answer was whether her Vision was important enough to merit going back to school to achieve it.

It's important to note that there is no judgment here, no right or wrong. What is worthwhile to one person simply may not be worthwhile to someone else. And that leads us directly to the next point: Having a worthy Vision is essential, but that alone is not enough. The Vision must also be worthy to *you*. It must be yours – not someone else's dream for you or expectations of you. Just because your doctor or your spouse thinks it would be beneficial for you to get more exercise doesn't necessarily make it important to you.

It's easy to fall into the trap of pursuing a dream or trying to make a change because someone else thinks you should or because you want to please someone who is special to you. But despite potential good intentions on everyone's part, you will have a difficult time staying motivated unless *you* have a strong desire to change. This doesn't mean you can't be motivated to make changes that other people want you to make; it just means you have to get in touch with why the change is important to you personally.

Motivate me

In the space below, write down several worthwhile pursuits – some changes you've been wanting to make in your life.

_____

_____

_____

_____

_____

_____

_____

Make the Vision Clear

Clarity is motivating. The clearer you are about the change you want to implement in your life, the more motivated you will be to make that change … and the more likely you will be to accomplish it. It may seem obvious that if you have a Vision, then you must be clear about it, right? Oftentimes what we think is our Vision is really a mask for a broader underlying desire. Let me share an example.

In my speeches and workshops I'm often asked, "Can the Vision be something like putting $1 million in the bank?" The answer is that the Vision can be anything you want it to be, so long as it is worthwhile to you. The problem with Visions like this, however, is that they are very often a means to an end rather than a true desired end state. If having $1 million in the bank were your Vision, what would that mean to you? Would it mean you wouldn't have to worry about paying your bills? Then your true vision is likely financial security. Would having $1 million make you feel successful? If so, then you may be seeking a feeling of accomplishment or self-worth.

You must understand exactly what it is you desire. If having $1 million is what you think you want when financial security is what you truly seek, you will quickly lose your motivation to acquire some arbitrary amount of money. Furthermore, even if you save $1 million, you still may not feel secure. This is precisely why clarity is so vital and so powerful.

Take a moment to review the list of worthwhile pursuits you wrote down in the previous section. Are you 100 percent clear about each of them? Do you need to take time to consider some of them at a deeper level and perhaps rethink what they mean to you?

Pick Just One Vision ... For Now

In his article "Will and Desire," Eknath Easwaran writes that a person's desire can be compared to a river. If the person has many desires, it is like the trickling of many little creeks, flowing all over the place with no direction. He contrasts this with a person with one all-consuming desire who can be compared to a mighty river. Like the Colorado River that carved the Grand Canyon out of solid rock, so too can a person with a focused desire do miraculous things.

Your highest level of motivation will result from having one worthwhile, intensely felt desire. If you spread yourself too thin by trying to focus on multiple Visions at once, you will likely have trouble being successful in any of them. You need to pick one Vision, one path, and follow it and reject other paths. You can't walk down two paths at once. If you walk down one path for awhile and then another path for awhile, guess what? You'll never get down either one. This doesn't mean you will always be doing the same thing. There can be variety in what you do, but each action should move you farther down the chosen path, bringing you closer to the final destination, your Vision.

Staying on one path is difficult for me, and it may be for you, too. Making a commitment to one Vision is hard for those who want to experiment and experience different things. Some might say that I am easily distracted, but I prefer to see myself as curious … extremely curious. I've dabbled in writing screenplays, digital video editing, nature photography, classical guitar and building stained-glass windows. My most recent pursuit was teaching myself options trading. Options trading is complicated, and it can be financially dangerous if you don't educate yourself thoroughly. The most dangerous thing about it for me, however, was that it took time away from my Vision — becoming the expert on self-motivation.

Committing to one worthwhile and clearly defined Vision keeps me from squandering my time on other pursuits and makes me more successful in achieving my Vision. I don't mean to suggest that we should have one-track lives. My life is about more than becoming the expert on self-motivation. But that Vision must be my priority in order for it to happen. So, I spend some time on my photography hobby, but I'm no longer pursuing options trading.

Perhaps you also have many different worthwhile pursuits or dreams. For now, I strongly suggest you choose only one Vision on which to focus. Choose the one you are willing to commit to — the one that means the most, that you are most passionate about or that would have the biggest impact on your life. Once you fully understand the VSE model and have learned how to apply it to your life, then *perhaps* you can work on more than one Vision and create a Motivation Plan for each. For example, if your Vision was to lose 50 pounds, that would be best done over a period of time. Once you've created your Motivation Plan and are successfully following it, you might be able to simultaneously pursue a Vision such as getting a part in a local theater production.

I know myself well enough to understand that I will fall off the wagon again and start on yet another fascinating pursuit. It's who I am. But because I choose to be *intentional*, I also know I will eventually realize that the pursuit is taking up time that I need to be spending on my Vision. And because my Vision is worthwhile to me, I will be motivated to get back on track and follow my highest path.

Motivate *me*

Write down the one Vision you will focus on for now – the one that means the most to you, that you are most passionate about or that would have the biggest impact on your life.

_____

_____

_____

Valuing the Vision

Now that you have clearly identified your Vision, there are several strategies you can use to maximize the motivational power of that Vision.

 **Strategy: Focus on the "Whys"**

Identifying the reasons why your Vision is important fuels your passion. When you have a genuine and unwavering purpose, you will be willing to do the necessary work to achieve the Vision and to tolerate any discomfort and unpleasantness it may entail. In short, the "whys" will help keep you motivated. The key to this strategy is to write down all the benefits that achieving your Vision will create in your life.

For example, let's assume your Vision is to find a new job. First, determine how worthwhile this Vision is by asking yourself, "How important is finding a new job to me? Am I willing to put forth the effort to create a new résumé, look for openings, follow through with the interview process and actually switch jobs?"

Then, write down all the benefits a different job will bring. Will it pay more? Will there be more prestige? Will it be more interesting and fulfilling? Will there be more job security or more potential growth?

Why is it important to write these reasons down? So you can use the written words as tools to keep yourself motivated. When you don't feel like working on your résumé or you become discouraged in your job search, looking at your whys will often give you the nudge you need to get going again.

Vision

Motivate *me*

Write down all the reasons why your Vision is important to you.

_____
_____
_____
_____
_____
_____
_____
_____

Strategy: Do a "Cost Analysis"

In economics, there is a concept known as "opportunity cost" – the cost of *not* doing something. We can use the same concept in self-motivation by identifying the "costs" of not realizing our Vision, that is, the potential negative impact on your life if you don't make this change. The idea is that when we become aware of these costs, we are more likely to be motivated to change our behaviors and actions.

Using the previous example in which the Vision is to find a new job, what might the costs be of *not* achieving that Vision? If your present job is highly stressful, the costs could be any number of health consequences. If your present job requires long hours or a great deal of travel, the costs could be irreparable damage to your relationship with your significant other. If your present company is being sold or experiencing financial problems, the cost could be that you end up without a job at all.

Sometimes, our "whys" are simply not powerful enough to motivate us to achieve our Vision. That's when we need to look at the consequences of not achieving it. We are often more inclined to make a change when the pain of staying the same is greater than the effort of changing.

Motivate *me*

Write down the "costs" to you – both literally and figuratively – of not manifesting your Vision.

_____
_____
_____
_____
_____

Strategy: Replace Rather Than Eliminate

One of the most powerful principles of change management is to *replace rather than eliminate*. In other words, instead of eliminating a non-desired behavior, replace it with a desired behavior.

As an example, my wife thought we were eating too much animal protein. She wanted to institute a "policy" of two non-meat days. That sounded rather harsh to me. I suggested instead that we institute a policy of two vegetarian days. It seems like it shouldn't be that important, but when I eliminated the negative "meatless days" and replaced it with "vegetarian days," I immediately started thinking of different recipes we could use to implement this new approach. No longer was I depriving myself of meat. Instead, I was looking for opportunities: "Let's see if we can make that tofu curry with pineapple that we always order at the Thai restaurant."

Replacing is more powerful than eliminating for several reasons:

1. Elimination feels like deprivation;
2. Nature abhors a vacuum – if you simply eliminate a behavior, there's no telling what will replace it;
3. Replacing opens you up to exploring possibilities.

This principle holds true with self-motivation, as well. The Vision is a change you want to make that will improve your life. These changes are often things we want to eliminate or stop doing – stop smoking, stop eating too much, stop being a couch potato, stop getting into abusive relationships. Stopping something is rarely motivating.

To maximize your motivation, position your Vision as a positive replacement for that behavior or situation you want to eliminate. *Stop smoking* becomes *improve my health*. *Stop eating too much* could be *lower cholesterol* or *lose 10 pounds*. *Stop being a couch potato* might be replaced with *compete in a biathlon*. *Stop getting into abusive relationships* becomes *find a mate who respects me and loves me for who I am*.

Strategy: Write Your Vision as an Affirmation and Visualize it Every Day

An affirmation is a declaration that a situation – in this case, your Vision – is already true even though it has not yet become reality. There are countless articles, blogs and books about the power of affirmations and visualization and how to utilize them in your life. Affirmations help you focus your attention on what you desire, because what you focus on, you will achieve. They also reprogram your unconscious mind and open you up to a powerful belief in yourself.

A great book on the power of affirmations is Jack Canfield's *The Success Principles*. Jack describes the relationship between affirmations and motivation this way: "[Affirmations] create in the brain a dynamic tension that results in motivation. All motivation comes from having a picture of something that you want in your head that you have not yet created in reality. The purpose of an affirmation is to create and maintain this tension to create motivation."

When you state your Vision as an affirmation, you receive not only the motivational power inherent in having a worthwhile pursuit, but also the life changing power of affirmations. How do you write a good Vision-based affirmation?

- ❖ Use the present tense, as if the change has already occurred. Don't say, "I will" or "I'm going to." Instead say, "I am...."
- ❖ State it in the first person with "I" or "my."
- ❖ Express it in a positive way. Focus on what you want, rather than what you don't want. Instead of, "I don't lose my temper," say, "I am calm and in control."
- ❖ Use action-oriented phrases such as verbs ending in *-ing*.

❖ Make it clear and specific. Stating a specific dollar amount for the salary you want to make in your new job is better than simply saying you want to make more money.

As an example, my Vision stated as an affirmation is: *I am the self-motivation expert – making presentations, leading workshops, writing books and helping other people achieve their dreams.*

I suggest you write your Vision as an affirmation on several note cards. Then place the note cards where you will see them several times a day – on your bathroom mirror, on the refrigerator, in your car. Every time you see a note card, state your Vision out loud.

The second part of this strategy involves visualizing your Vision affirmation every day. Visualizing programs your brain for success, opens your mind to the resources available to you and builds your belief. Experts suggest visualizing your Vision at least once a day. When you visualize, vividly imagine your Vision as if you have already achieved it, using all your senses and feeling the emotions you would experience.

The Vision Drives Commitment

In 2004, Maria Sharapova defeated Serena Williams to take the Wimbledon title at the age of 17. People talked about her "coming out of nowhere" and how she had amazing talent and great genes. There's no denying she has talent, and her height of 6'2" helps, too, but consider what she did to manifest her potential. At age 7, she left her home in Russia and moved to the United States for professional coaching. She spent the next 10 years preparing for that day at Wimbledon. Almost 60 percent of her life was focused on her Vision to be one of the world's greatest tennis players.

A clear, worthwhile Vision drives commitment. Committing yourself means making a promise to yourself – a promise to actively participate in your life, to fully develop your potential, to put in the work required for success and to persist. It would seem obvious that we need commitment and hard work to achieve our Vision, but many people think they deserve to succeed "just because." Commitment and hard work will get you where you want to go. Without it, you simply aren't going to go far.

What is so fascinating about commitment and hard work is that they become a bit addictive, and hopefully, they become a habit. As you begin to see positive results, your effort becomes easier and even enjoyable. When I first started taking lessons to learn how to play classical guitar, I told my teacher I only had time to practice 10 minutes a night. He was smart, and he was getting paid, so he just nodded his head. Well, I practiced every night the first month at least 10 minutes, and often I had to force myself to keep going. But after a couple of months, those 10 minutes stretched into 20, and then 30 and not uncommonly into an hour. My commitment to practice, even for 10 minutes, paid off and gave me success. As a result, I was motivated to practice even more.

One of my favorite quotes about commitment is by Johann Wolfgang von Goethe. The last sentences are the most famous, but the earlier lines are just as important:

> *Until one is committed there is hesitancy,*
> *a chance to draw back, always ineffectiveness.*
> *Concerning all acts of initiative and creation,*
>   *there is one elementary truth,*
> *the ignorance of which kills countless ideas and splendid plans;*
> *that the moment that one definitely commits oneself,*
>   *then providence moves, too.*

*All sorts of things occur to help one that would never
   otherwise have occurred.*
*A whole stream of events issues from the decision,
   raising in one's favor*
*all manner of unforeseen incidents, meetings and
   material assistance,*
which no man could have dreamed would come his way.
Whatever you can do, or dream you can, begin it!
Boldness has genius, power and magic in it.
Begin it now!

Today, I invite you to commit to your worthwhile Vision and begin living the life of your dreams.

SUMMARY

❖ The Vision must be worthwhile to you.

❖ The clearer you are about the change you want to implement in your life, the more motivated you will be to make that change and the more likely you will be to accomplish it.

❖ Your highest level of motivation will result from having one worthwhile, intensely felt desire.

❖ Strategies to maximize the motivational power of the Vision:
  ✦ Focus on the "whys"
  ✦ Do a cost analysis
  ✦ Replace rather than eliminate
  ✦ Write your Vision as an affirmation and visualize it every day

❖ Commit to your Vision and be prepared to work.

iMotivate*me*

three

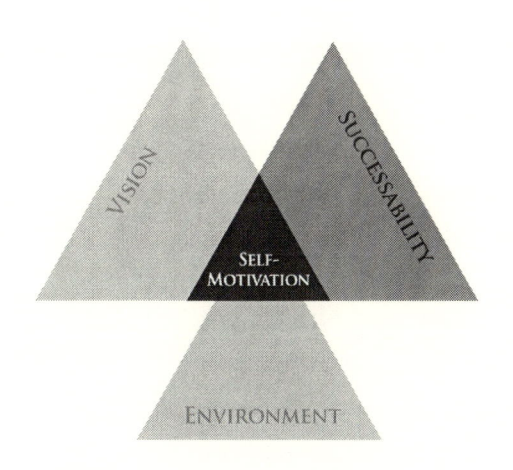

Successability

Now that you've identified your Vision, we're going to address the second factor in the VSE triad: Successability.

What is Successability?

Successability is your confidence in your competence, that is, how confident you are in your abilities. Successability refers to your confidence in two different realms. The first is how confident you are in general – how effectively you think you handle all that life throws at you. The second is how confident you are in your ability to achieve your Vision. The more confident you are in your ability to succeed, the more motivated you will be.

The opposite of Successability is *amotivation*, a term coined by Edward Deci in *The Psychology of Self-Determination*, which means a sense of futility. An amotivated person thinks he is not capable of doing something that he feels he is expected to do. If there is a particular goal you desire, but in your heart of hearts you think that you will not be able to achieve it, you will not be motivated to go after it. It follows, of course, that if you don't go after it, you are guaranteed not to achieve it.

> **Successability**
> Your confidence in your competence – your ability to achieve your Vision.

In his article "Self-Efficacy" in the *Encyclopedia of Human Behavior*, Albert Bandura, a professor of psychology at Stanford University, explains the major differences between people who are confident in their abilities and those who are not:

1. Confident people approach difficult tasks as challenges and, in fact, look forward to accomplishing them, while non-confident people perceive difficult tasks as threats and shy away from them.

2. Confident people are able to maintain sustained effort in meeting challenges. Rather than seeing setbacks and failures as devastating, they quickly recover and proceed toward their objective. Non-confident people see themselves as incompetent when setbacks or failures occur, and they tend to give up.

3. Confident people have lower stress because of their confidence in their ability to deal with situations that may arise. Non-confident people easily become stressed and depressed because of their perceived lack of control over events.

4. Confident people set higher goals for themselves and are more committed to achieving them. On the other hand, non-confident people tend to do and be the opposite.

The result of these differences is that those who are more confident are able to accomplish so much more in their lives. Clearly, we want to be confident people! As Henry David Thoreau said, "I have learned that if one advances confidently in the direction of his dreams, and endeavors to live the life he has imagined, he will meet with a success unexpected in common hours."

I want you to be a person who advances confidently in the direction of your Vision. But what if you aren't such a person? If one has low self-confidence, is that person stuck forever with low motivation? Absolutely not! But encouraging someone to "be more confident" isn't very helpful, is it? What we need are specific behaviors that will result in our being more confident.

Research shows that two factors in particular increase our confidence in our competence: **clarity** and **control**. The purpose of this and the next chapter is to examine these factors and to provide you with strategies that will positively impact your Successability.

Clarity

Clarity means knowing exactly *what* you want to accomplish and *how* you are going to achieve it. We can't feel confident we will be successful if we don't even know what success entails. Nor can we feel confident we will be successful if we don't know how to achieve that success.

The more clarity you have, the more motivated you will be. When faced with a new pursuit, it's natural to be unsure as to what the first and subsequent steps should be. But when we are uncertain, we become hesitant and unmotivated, and before you know it, we're stopped dead in our tracks.

Clarity enhances confidence because you know where you're going, how you're going to get there and what the next step should be. One of the best strategies for creating clarity is to get information out of your head and into a tangible form. Your mind is a good place to ponder ideas, concepts and action steps. However, until you get them down on paper, they are not concrete or definite – they are subject to your memory, your perceptions and your biases. In addition, putting ideas in written form makes it easier to see connections between them, establish priorities and develop a logical order.

To achieve clarity in any endeavor, write your thoughts down, either on a computer or in a journal. It is precisely because clarity is such a powerful motivator that many of the strategies and exercises in this book involve writing something down.

Strategy: Know Your Strengths

Each of us has unique strengths, talents, abilities and special gifts. Strengths can include natural abilities, knowledge you've acquired, skills you've developed and experience you've gained. When we understand, acknowledge and appreciate our strengths, they grow. When we deny our strengths, they wither away. Clearly understanding your strengths increases your Successability, your motivation and, ultimately, the likelihood of manifesting your Vision.

What are your strengths, special talents and positive attributes? What can you do to further enhance each of these? Spend some time today thinking about the gifts you have been given and ways you can nurture and grow those gifts.

Strategy: Examine Your Self-Imposed Limitations and Self-Fulfilling Prophecies

Self-imposed limitations and self-fulfilling prophecies can wreak havoc on your Successability. A self-imposed limitation is the belief that you lack a skill, characteristic or trait necessary to achieve your Vision. That missing ingredient could be wisdom, good looks, the ability to speak well, contacts, resources or a specific skill. Self-imposed limitations are often announced or prefaced with the word "but." For example, "I want to be a screenwriter, *but* I don't know anyone in the business," or, "I'd like to be a clinical social worker, *but* I wouldn't make enough money to support myself." Sometimes our history can be the source of a self-limiting belief, such as, "I never finish what I start." Other times, our perception of negative inherited traits can be a self-imposed limitation, as in, "The nut doesn't fall far from the tree."

Self-fulfilling prophecies also negatively impact Successability. In his book, *Social Theory and Social Structure*, Robert K. Merton defines a self-fulfilling prophecy as "in the beginning, a false definition of a situation, evoking a new behavior which makes the originally false conception come true." My favorite example of a self-fulfilling prophecy is the supposed story about an American woman who was adopting a Chinese baby. In preparation for the wonderful day when the child would arrive, she decided to learn Chinese so she could communicate with the child when it started to talk. The baby arrived, and the mother only spoke Chinese to it, so of course the baby grew up speaking Chinese. The mom was very happy she had the foresight to learn Chinese!

This is a silly story, but so too are many of the self-fulfilling prophecies we act out every day. How many of us have thought or said the words, "With my luck..." and then predicted some horrendous outcome? Or perhaps with respect to a suggested solution we've said, "I'll give it a try, but I don't think it will work"?

Our self-imposed limitations and self-fulfilling prophecies have great power to alter the outcome of a given situation. They cause us to shortchange ourselves by creating our own obstacles. Life throws enough obstacles our way that we don't need to create more for ourselves!

I have a friend, we'll call her Janie, who sees herself as a person who can't follow through. Every time Janie gets about two weeks into a new project, she starts to question her ability to stick with it, focusing on the same three projects she didn't complete some time in the distant past. An honest examination of her beliefs and self-fulfilling prophecy revealed to her that she was totally ignoring the many projects she had successfully completed, as well as the extenuating circumstances that led her to not complete the three albatross projects.

We need to honestly examine our self-defeating messages, determine if they are valid and figure out what we can do about them. What self-imposed limitations or self-fulfilling prophecies might prevent you from manifesting your Vision? Are they real or are they falsehoods that you've learned to use as a crutch? What is the truth about your abilities and expectancies?

The strategy for dealing with these self-imposed obstacles is to act with intention, to operate in that uniquely human space between stimulus and action. You can either expect the worst or expect the best. It's your choice. Try expecting the best out of yourself and the situation and see what happens!

Strategy: Discover Your Stories of Achievement

Another strategy for increasing your confidence in your ability to achieve your Vision is remembering past experiences in which you were extremely competent – experiences in which you succeeded beyond any doubt. Identifying, reliving and writing down these stories of achievement increases clarity because it opens your belief system to the fact that you do have what it takes to achieve your Vision.

Sadly, most of us are much more likely to dwell upon experiences in which we failed or to remember the goals we haven't achieved rather than celebrate our successes. Some of our victories we simply forget; others we discount as "no big deal." Is it any wonder that we often doubt our ability to achieve our Vision?

As intentional men and women, *we have the power to choose which experiences we will identify with*, and we need to choose our stories of achievement. We all have these stories; some of us might have to work a little harder to dig them out. My favorite stories of achievement are completing my baccalaureate thesis on the bifurcated economy of Hong Kong, winning the Toastmasters International Speech contest in my division, and giving a presentation early in my career on human sexuality and the law. Even today as I write about these successes, some more than 20 years ago, they still motivate me. When doubts start to creep in, wreaking havoc on my motivation, remembering them brings my Successability back in line.

Motivate *me*

Take some quiet time to think of two or three experiences from your life of which you are especially proud. Consider situations that reflect positively on your character, talents or skills. The stories don't necessarily have to relate to your Vision, but if they do, all the better. Relive these stories of achievement in your mind, complete with details. Then, in the spaces below, write down a phrase or sentence to describe each one.

1. _____
2. _____
3. _____

Control

It is a basic human tendency to seek to control our lives and our environment. Exercising control over our lives is inherently motivating, while feeling that we lack control is a powerful de-motivator. We perceive that we are in control when we can see a clear cause-and-effect relationship between our actions and a desired end result.

Of course, there are some things in life we just can't control, but those rarely determine our success. When veteran television announcer Charlie Jones was assigned to cover Olympic rowing, canoeing and kayaking, he prepared for the broadcast by interviewing some of the athletes. Asking what they would do in case of rain, strong winds or choppy water, their response was always the same: "That's outside my boat." After hearing that answer again and again, Charlie realized these Olympic athletes were interested only in what they could control, which was what happened inside their boat. Everything else was beyond their control and not worth expending any mental or physical energy on.

How much confidence and motivation would these athletes have had if they had believed Olympic glory rested primarily on the sheer luck of weather and water conditions on the day of the event? Not much! On the other hand, consider how confident and motivated they were, knowing that achieving their Vision of winning an Olympic medal was primarily within their control.

Strategy: Focus on What You Can Control

David Brooks, a World Champion of Public Speaking, has said that when he made the decision to be the champion, he knew he wasn't the best speaker, so he knew he would have to be the best prepared. David understood that he couldn't control whether he was the most gifted or talented speaker. He focused instead on what he could control: how prepared he was. By focusing on what he could control and letting go of what he couldn't, he instinctively motivated himself.

No matter your Vision, there are certain elements that you can control through your decisions, your choices and your actions. Stop for a moment and think about your Vision. Which aspects or elements of it do you have control over? Focus on those and don't allow yourself to become absorbed by the few things you can't control.

Strategy: Enhance Your Abilities

An often quoted comment about motivation goes as follows: "Ability is what you can do; motivation is what you will do." This is true, so far as it goes. However, we need to be clear as to what we mean when we discuss "ability," because ability has two components:

1. Your *present ability* – what you are able to do now, that is, your present skill set, knowledge and experience;

2. Your *potential ability* – what you could do if you enhanced, supplemented or increased your present skill set, knowledge and experience.

With some self-examination, it's not unusual to discover that you may not have the ability to achieve your Vision. Perhaps you are missing some knowledge or one or more necessary skills. When you think about it, this isn't surprising. This missing ability may be the very reason you haven't yet manifested your Vision. But **don't let your present ability rob you of your motivation or keep you from being all that you can be, especially when your potential ability is so great.**

So how can you tap into and develop your potential ability? First, you must identify the discrepancies between your present abilities and those you need in order to manifest your Vision. Are there certain skills you must have? Do you need to gain some experience in a new field? Try not to think of the issue as how you are deficient, but rather, in what ways you haven't yet grown enough to achieve your Vision. In other words, view these issues not as weaknesses but as developmental opportunities. Take some time with this very important first step. Only by identifying those things that might prevent you from achieving your Vision can you address them.

The next step is to identify resources that will help you enhance your developmental opportunities. The good news is there are many resources, people and organizations that are available to help you grow and develop. You can increase your skill set through both formal and informal training. Examples include:

- ❖ **Your job** – find out if your employer offers training programs or workshops.

- ❖ **Educational facilities** such as local universities, community colleges and trade/technical schools.

- ❖ **On-line classes or training** – these can be completed in your own home, at a time that is convenient for you.

- ❖ **Other training venues** such as public seminars and continuing education classes.

- ❖ **Informal training** and skill development can come from trade associations, networking groups, support groups and mentors/coaches. Toastmasters has played a large part in helping me hone my speaking skills. I am also a member of a marketing group. Through its newsletter and interactions with other members, I've learned the skills I need to market myself as a speaker and an author.

You can enhance your knowledge by reading books, listening to experts or doing research. Expand your experience level by getting away from your desk, taking risks and trying different things. Find an organization where you can practice the traits you need to develop. For example, if your Vision is to be a salesperson but you think you are too shy to speak to people, join a social business club and learn in a safe environment how to mingle.

iMotivateme

Motivate *me*

Identify any discrepancies between your present abilities and those you need in order to manifest your Vision. Then write down any skills you need to develop further and at least one way you can enhance those skills.

_____
_____
_____
_____
_____

Strategy: Create Success Experiences

You probably won't be surprised to learn that success builds self-confidence. You can increase your *expectancy for future success* (Successability) by increasing your *experiences with success*. One way to do this is to intentionally give yourself challenges that you can overcome. I call these *success experiences*. Every time you successfully face and overcome a challenge, your confidence in your competence grows. And when your confidence grows, so does your motivation.

Psychologist Albert Bandura, in his paper "Self-Efficacy," wrote that the most effective way to make people believe they can succeed is by giving them experiences in which they are successful. He points out, however, that if people experience only easy successes, they come to expect that success is easy, which results in them not being able to handle difficult situations. Experiencing more difficult successes, on the other hand, builds resilience and teaches us that success is a result of sustained effort. Hard work and struggle, Bandura tells us, make us stronger.

Recently, I watched this principle in action. After completing a workout session with my trainer, a new client showed up for training. The new client was an older gentleman who appeared to have health challenges. I perceived that he was extremely uncertain about his physical abilities. Every exercise my trainer gave the man challenged him but was within his ability. The man was never allowed to fail, and with every success I could actually see his motivation grow.

If you want to motivate yourself, and keep yourself motivated, create success experiences for yourself. Intentionally put yourself in situations that will challenge you and in which you can blossom. For example, if your Vision was to run a marathon, you would create a series of increasingly difficult steps, each of which you could achieve in turn:

1. Walk a half-marathon;
2. Run/walk a half-marathon;
3. Run/walk a full marathon;
4. Run a marathon.

As you successfully achieve each step, your confidence in your ability to achieve the next step grows. Creating success experiences teaches you that although you may not be able to control everything in life, you do in fact have significant control over the biggest factor in your success – your own actions.

Clarity and control are the keys to Successability, to increasing your confidence in your competence. In the next chapter, I will teach you a "super strategy" that will address these factors and turbocharge your Successability and, therefore, your motivation.

SUMMARY

❖ Successability is your confidence in your competence – how confident you are in your ability to achieve your Vision. The greater your Successability, the more motivated you will be.

❖ Two things in particular increase Successability:

1. Clarity – knowing exactly what you want to accomplish and how you are going to achieve it

    ✦ Strategy: Know your strengths

    ✦ Strategy: Examine your self-imposed limitations and self-fulfilling prophecies

    ✦ Strategy: Discover your stories of achievement

2. Control – exercising control over your life is inherently motivating

    ✦ Strategy: Focus on what you can control

    ✦ Strategy: Enhance your abilities

    ✦ Strategy: Create success experiences

four

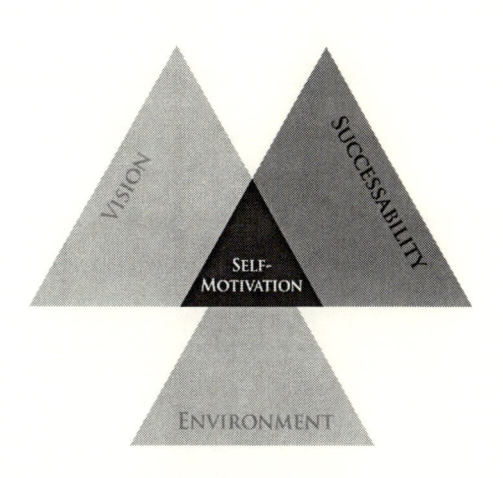

Successability: Divide & Conquer

Some Visions are so "big" that achieving them can be complex and feel overwhelming. Our confidence suffers ... and we wonder *if* we will be able to accomplish the Vision let alone *how* we will do it, and we quickly lose our motivation.

The solution is to "divide and conquer" – to break the Vision down into smaller, more manageable pieces in order to increase clarity and control. This Divide and Conquer strategy is so powerful and so crucial to your self-motivation that I call it a "super strategy" and will devote an entire chapter to it. Even if your Vision isn't particularly audacious, the Divide and Conquer strategy is essential because it will show you exactly *how* to achieve your Vision.

The concept of breaking large projects or ideas into component pieces is not rocket science. It's common sense ... but not necessarily common practice. We inherently know we should do it, but it's rarely done in a methodical, systematic way. The Divide and Conquer strategy is a step-by-step process for breaking your Vision into goals and tasks in order to increase your Successability. You will identify all the goals that must be achieved in order to manifest your Vision and all the tasks that must be completed in order to achieve each goal. If you complete the necessary tasks, the goals will be met (assuming your choice of tasks was accurate). If your goals are met, then your Vision will become reality (assuming your choice of goals was correct).

The Divide and Conquer strategy will also guide you in creating a Successability Blueprint™ – a written plan for achieving your Vision, including goals, tasks, priorities and timelines. The Blueprint provides immense clarity, and we know that clarity enhances confidence. After all, if you don't have a clear idea of what you must do, how can you feel confident about doing it? And what could be clearer than a list of tasks that you can refer to anytime you lose focus? With this strategy, you will always know exactly what you need to do next to achieve the Vision.

Breaking the Vision down and creating a Blueprint also gives you more control. The tasks represent observable behaviors – the specific actions that you will take. You cannot directly control the Vision, nor can you directly control the goals, but you can control your behaviors. For example, let's presume your Vision is to lose 50 pounds. Losing 50 pounds is not an observable behavior, nor is it something you can directly control. However, you can control your food choices for breakfast, lunch and dinner. You can observe yourself exercising for 20 minutes three times each week. You can count calories and take a fat-burning supplement. By focusing on the tasks, which you *can* control, you will increase your motivation.

The rest of this chapter will take you through the six steps of the Divide and Conquer strategy. At the end, I will walk you through the process of creating your own Successability Blueprint. Creating a Blueprint is perhaps the most important thing you can do to achieve your Vision and getting the plan on paper is a must. However, it will require some effort and self-discipline, because the structure will not come from someone else; it will be created by you. In *Your Own Worst Enemy: Breaking the Habit of Adult Underachievement*, Kenneth Christian writes, "Creating a path where none exists requires skill and self-discipline." Rest assured, however, that the results will be well worth the effort as you gain the confidence to pursue and achieve your dreams.

Step 1: Break the Vision Down into Manageable Goals

A goal is an accomplishment, the achievement of which will move you closer to realizing your Vision. Most Visions will require several, possibly many, goals. Typically, there are numerous ways to manifest a Vision – different paths you can take, so to speak. As you choose your way and identify and write down your goals, make certain that each goal absolutely (not probably) moves you toward your Vision.

To optimize your motivation, keep your goals challenging but attainable. If you don't believe you can achieve a goal, you won't be motivated to try. For example, it's not realistic to think you can run a 10K race a month from now if you haven't exercised in several years. However, don't necessarily reject a goal that will move you toward your Vision because it's a stretch for you (or conversely, because it's easy). The point is to be intentional.

Many goal-setting experts talk about the value of setting "SMART" goals – goals that are Specific, Measurable, Attainable, Realistic and Timely. While I agree with this concept and its inherent value, if you focus too much on creating SMART goals at this point, you run the risk of getting bogged down and losing your motivation. One of the key purposes of the Divide and Conquer strategy is to move you from a broad Vision to specific, measurable, time-driven tasks, so in essence you will use this process to create SMART tasks.

With that said, your goals should be clearly stated and easily understood. If a goal is vague, it will not motivate you. For example, if your Vision were to get a new job, a goal to "network" is too general. A better goal would be something like, "Network with other sales professionals at local events and national conferences."

When I divided my Vision into manageable goals, it looked like this:

VISION: I am the self-motivation expert – making presentations, leading workshops, writing books and helping other people achieve their dreams.

> **Goal:** Earn my Distinguished Toastmaster certification (DTM)
> **Goal:** Write and publish a book on self-motivation
> **Goal:** Develop and present a speech on self-motivation
> **Goal:** Expand speech into hands-on workshop on self-motivation
> **Goal:** Partake of opportunities to speak in different forums
> **Goal:** Market my book, workshop and speech

Step 2: Prioritize Your Goals

Prioritizing your goals focuses your energy and helps you create a logical order for accomplishing them. How you prioritize is often dependent on the nature of your Vision. In some cases, one goal will be a condition precedent to another goal, that is, you need to achieve one goal before you can achieve another. This makes prioritizing your goals easy because you simply put them in the correct sequence. In my case, I had to create the book, workshop and speech before I could market them. In the job search example from above, you would have to create or update your résumé before going to a job fair or applying for specific positions.

Other times, the priorities may not be so obvious. Let's assume that one of the goals for your job search was to do some networking. Should you start networking as soon as possible (networking is the top priority) or wait until your résumé is done (résumé is the top priority)? Either one could be right.

If there is no logical priority, consider choosing as your first few goals ones that you can achieve quickly, are relatively easy or will be fun. Remember the Create Success Experiences strategy from the last chapter? Success builds confidence and motivation. If you like networking and dread working on your résumé, get out there and start networking! Get some early successes that will generate momentum and keep you motivated.

Sometimes it will be necessary to work on more than one goal at the same time, for instance when you are waiting on someone else to complete something you need before you can continue. But try to avoid working on too many goals at once, as it can drain your energy and leave you unfocused. This will negatively impact your Successability, robbing you of your motivation.

Step 3: Break Each Goal into Tasks and Subtasks

If goals are the accomplishments by which you manifest your Vision, tasks are the activities by which you accomplish your goals.

This is where your Vision comes to fruition — in the small steps we call tasks. A task is an observable behavior — we can see someone doing a task.

Dividing goals into bite-size pieces, each of which can be "conquered" without a great deal of difficulty, provides even more clarity and control. And as you accomplish the tasks, perhaps daily, you pave your path with many successes. As a result, your Successability will quickly grow, sustaining your motivation.

If a goal is complex or will involve many steps, it may be necessary to divide its tasks even further into subtasks. You can do this either by breaking the task into its component parts or by limiting the amount of time you will work on that particular task. As you may recall, one of my goals is to market my book, workshop and speech. I broke that goal down into many different tasks, and one of those tasks was to develop a following on Twitter. (Follow me @BobPrentiss.) Even that seemed a bit overwhelming, so I broke that task into subtasks, one of which was to purchase and read a book on how to use Twitter for marketing.

When the book came in the mail, the first thing I noticed was how long it was — 477 pages. The very next thing I noticed was that the lawn needed mowing. I was clearly looking for a distraction, some reason to not read the book. I knew I wanted to become knowledgeable about Twitter, but my motivation wasn't strong enough to tackle a 477-page book. So I broke the task into subtasks by setting a time limit to read for one hour. I even set a timer so I wouldn't be distracted wondering when I'd completed my hour, and I told myself that after that hour if I still wanted to mow the lawn, I would do it. With a much more manageable task, one I was confident I could complete, I was once again motivated. As it turned out, I studied the book for an hour and then just kept reading for another hour.

> **VISION: I am the self-motivation expert – making presentations, leading workshops, writing books and helping other people achieve their dreams.**
>
> **Goal:** Earn my Distinguished Toastmaster certification (DTM)
> **Goal:** Write and publish a book on self-motivation
> **Goal:** Develop and present a workshop on self-motivation
> **Goal:** Develop and present a speech on self-motivation
> **Goal:** Partake of opportunities to speak in different forums
> **Goal:** Market my book, workshop and speech
>   Task: Join a marketing mastermind group
>   Task: Get a publicist
>   Task: Start a blog
>   Task: Develop a following on Twitter
>   ✦ Purchase and read a book on how to use Twitter for marketing
>   ✧ Read for one hour each day
>   ✦ Follow others who are succeeding on Twitter

This example illustrates just one more reason why the Divide and Conquer strategy is so powerful: It matches the task to your available motivation. I didn't have enough motivation to read the whole darn book, but I did have enough to read for one hour, which turned into two hours. I just as easily could have divided the task of studying the book into subtasks by assigning myself a certain number of chapters to read in each sitting. Breaking tasks down, either by component part or by setting time limits, can work wonders when you are facing an overwhelmingly big task.

Using the Divide and Conquer strategy to create a Successability Blueprint is motivating because it builds your belief that you can in fact achieve your Vision ... and you get excited about doing so. But we all know that enthusiasm will eventually wear off. So we want to make sure that our tasks and subtasks are motivating. Motivating tasks are:

- ❖ **Clear and Specific** – They must be easily understood and written with detail. If you are confused as to exactly what you are supposed to do, you will not be motivated.

- ❖ **Observable** – Tasks and subtasks are behaviors, something you can see.

- ❖ **Measurable** – Each task should have a clearly defined result or outcome so that you can measure your progress and determine when you have accomplished it.

- ❖ **Realistic** – You must believe you can perform the task, otherwise, you won't be motivated to do it. Complex tasks should be broken down into smaller component tasks.

Step 4: Create a Timeline

A timeline focuses your forward movement and allows you to evaluate your progress. If you don't set a definite time to begin working toward your Vision, the commitment is too vague. You believe you can start at any time, so there's no urgency to take action now. Furthermore, without a completion date, it's too easy to let things drag on. Putting an endpoint on your Vision gives you a clear target to work toward.

Attaching a timeline to your goals and tasks forces you to give some serious thought to how long it will realistically take to achieve the Vision. Having an honest assessment of the time involved is motivating – no matter how long that might be – because clarity is motivating. Of course, visions that can be accomplished in a relatively short period of time are inherently motivating because you know that if you stay on track, you will soon experience the reward and sense of accomplishment.

Timelines are crucial for long-term Visions. These are often the Visions that suffer the most from a loss of motivation. Even if you come to the realization (as I did) that it may take a year or more to achieve your Vision, if you follow your Successability Blueprint and keep to the timeline, you can be confident that you will achieve it. You know that there is a light at the end of the tunnel.

You may be wondering, "What if I set a completion date, but I don't accomplish the task or achieve the goal or Vision by that date?" Answer: You reset the date and adjust the rest of the timeline accordingly. As author Billy Cox says in *The Dream Book*, "If you were building a skyscraper and didn't finish on time, would you stop building? Of course not! You'd simply set a new deadline and get back to work." Well said.

How complex you make the timeline will vary. How complex is your Vision? Short-term and uncomplicated Visions need only a simple timeline. Longer-term and more complicated Visions may require more thought about how you can use your time most efficiently and effectively.

Step 5: Take Action

You should now have a clear plan for how to achieve your Vision. However, a plan is just a plan unless you implement it. You must take action. This is the point at which many people lose their motivation. Fortunately, the Divide and Conquer strategy addresses this.

To begin implementing your Successability Blueprint, print it out and mark with a highlighter the first three tasks that need attention. As you complete each task, cross through it on your printed copy and later enter the strike-through on the computer file. You want to strike through rather than delete completed tasks because seeing all that you have accomplished is highly motivating.

When you complete one task, highlight the next highest priority task so that you always have three tasks highlighted. This keeps your momentum going. Many people find it very effective to add the three highlighted tasks to their personal and/or professional weekly to-do list, thereby incorporating their work on their Vision into the their daily life.

For most people, the clarity and control the Successability Blueprint provides is very motivating. However, if your Blueprint is very detailed or your Vision very involved, it is possible that the number of tasks on the Blueprint may feel overwhelming. Keep in mind that these are the baby steps that will get you to your Vision. All you have to do is follow the plan.

Working through the tasks often results in needing to fine-tune the Blueprint. That's fine. It is supposed to be fluid and ever-changing (which is why creating it on a computer is very helpful). Write any changes on your printed copy and revise the computer version later.

> "It's not enough to be busy, so are the ants. The question is, what are we busy about?"
> - David Thoreau

The Successability Blueprint focuses your attention and allows you to judge how you're doing. Some people like to print the entire Blueprint so they can see the big picture; others prefer to print only the goal they are currently working toward; and some print out only the three highlighted tasks awaiting completion.

No matter which option you choose, you will want to **keep your Blueprint in view.** When you are ready to work on your Vision, all you need to do is look at your Successability Blueprint, and you will know exactly what needs to be done next.

While I was working toward my goal of developing a workshop, I was asked to give a presentation on a topic other than self-motivation. Because *partaking of opportunities to present* is another goal, I turned my attention away from the workshop and spent several weeks preparing for the speech. After the presentation, I knew it was time to get back to the workshop, but I wasn't motivated. I did just about anything else I could think of – installed a ceiling fan, washed the dog, watched a whole season of Scrubs. Finally, I decided to take my own advice and sat down with my Successability Blueprint. Once I had that in hand, I knew what I needed to do and I was motivated. In fact, I had self-motivated. That is the power of the Divide and Conquer strategy.

Step 6: Celebrate Your Successes

Some motivational experts recommend rewarding yourself for achieving tasks or goals. However, research tends to show that intrinsic motivation (that is, motivation from within, such as a feeling of accomplishment) is stronger than external motivation (motivation from outside of you, such as a reward).

So while I'm not sold on the idea of rewarding yourself for the completion of every task, I do believe that rewarding yourself for accomplishing major goals or especially challenging tasks can be motivational. (In fact, I'll share a strategy for this in a later chapter.) In addition, I think it is important to acknowledge your successful completion of a task, maybe even celebrate it, and celebrate yourself. (I actually reach my arm up over my opposite shoulder and pat myself on the back. Try it!) This acknowledgement increases your confidence in your capabilities and thereby increases your motivation to take on the next task ... and the next one ... until you have achieved your Vision.

SUMMARY

❖ The Divide and Conquer strategy and resulting Successability Blueprint show you exactly *how* you will achieve your Vision and provides clarity and control – the two keys to Successability. The six steps are:

    1. Break the Vision Down into Manageable Goals

    2. Prioritize Your Goals

    3. Break Each Goal into Tasks and Subtasks

    4. Create a Timeline

    5. Take Action

    6. Celebrate Your Successes

A Sample Successability Blueprint for Weight Loss

Now we can pull together all that we've learned so far about the Vision and Successability with a subject that is probably an issue for many of us: weight loss. I'm especially interested in this topic because I was fat as a kid, although my mother always lovingly referred to me as "husky." Let's see how one intentional woman – I'll refer to her as Stephanie – applied the VSE Model for Self-Motivation to losing weight.

Stephanie knew that the change she wanted to make in her life was to lose weight. Her Vision was certainly worthwhile. She wrote down her "whys." They were simple and powerful. Heart disease and diabetes were rampant in her family, so she wanted to do all that she could to prevent those diseases. Just as importantly, she wanted to be able to play ball and go hiking with her kids.

Stephanie decided that instead of focusing on *losing* weight, she would "replace rather than eliminate" and state her Vision in a positive manner. She considered: *Me at a Healthy Weight, Me Fitting into a Size 10* and *Me Liking My Body Image*. Ultimately, she wrote down her Vision as an affirmation that was short and to the point: *Me Slim*.

But at 45 pounds overweight, the Vision of *Me Slim* seemed overwhelming to Stephanie. She had tried a number of diets before and had lost weight but had always gained it back. Consequently, she was afraid the same thing would happen again this time. Instead of letting her fears stop her, she focused on the aspects of her Vision that she knew she could control right now – exercise and the food she chose to eat.

She also took the time to think about some Stories of Achievement. Stephanie knew that inside she was a slim woman, just as she'd been before her four children were born. She remembered that she used to be quite athletic and actually enjoyed exercising. She wrote down how she'd done aerobics up until a week before her first child was born and how quickly she was able to get her figure back.

Stephanie then broke this seemingly overwhelming Vision into manageable pieces using the Divide and Conquer strategy. And to keep her momentum going, every week she incorporated the next three tasks from her Successability Blueprint into her weekly to-do list. On the following page is Stephanie's Successability Blueprint with timeline:

STEPHANIE'S SUCCESSABILITY BLUEPRINT FOR BEING SLIM

VISION: ME SLIM
(which means lose the weight *and* keep it off)

GOAL: Lose 35 pounds – start date May 30
Task: Join Weight Watchers – June 3
- ✦ Find the three closest locations – May 30
- ✦ Attend meetings at each location – June 1-10
- ✦ Decide which meeting times work best with my schedule – June 2
- ✦ Choose and join the group I'm most comfortable with and that has the best times for my schedule – June 12

Task: Set date to achieve goal of losing 35 pounds – June 15
Task: Go to meetings – ongoing
Task: Follow the program – ongoing
Task: Make a friend in Weight Watchers – June 17

GOAL: Develop healthy eating habits – start date June 5
Task: Define healthy eating habits – June 7
Task: Eat junk food only one day a week – ongoing
- ✦ Determine which day I will eat junk food – June 7
- ✦ Define "junk food" so I'm sure I won't eat it the other days – June 7
- ✦ Make sure there is no junk food in my house except on junk food day, so I'm not tempted to blow my plan on non-junk food days – ongoing

Task: Keep healthy foods handy so I always have healthy foods to eat – ongoing
- ✦ Determine what healthy foods I like – June 10
- ✦ Buy the "healthy foods" – ongoing

iMotivateme

> ✦ Clean and prep any vegetables that need it so they are readily accessible to me – ongoing

GOAL: Exercise regularly – start date June 10

Task: Join a gym – June 30
> ✦ Make a list of four gyms to visit – June 15
>> Find gyms that are conveniently located – June 10
>> Talk to friends for recommendations – June 10-15
> ✦ Visit all four gyms (do NOT feel pressured to join until all visits are made) – June 15-30
> ✦ Pick the gym I want to join and make the best deal – June 30

Task: Decide what type of exercise I want to do – July 15
> ✦ Make a list of exercises that seem fun – June 10
> ✦ Find out where I can try them out – June 12
> ✦ Try them out – June 15-July 15
> ✦ Decide which one I like best and fits my needs – July 15

Task: Hire a trainer – July 25
> ✦ Discuss with gym staff my needs and which trainer would be best for me – July 15
> ✦ Interview three trainers – July 16-25
> ✦ Pick the one I like the best – July 25

Task: Get a walking partner (maybe my Weight Watchers friend?) – June 24

Task: Track my exercise with an exercise log – ongoing
> ✦ Buy an exercise log that fits my needs – June 20

GOAL: Set up a system of rewards for success – start date June 15

Task: Determine what rewards I would like and would motivate me – June 18

Task: Set criteria for earning rewards – June 20

Motivate *me*

Create a Successability Blueprint to Achieve Your Vision

I strongly suggest you complete the following steps on a computer. Using a computer allows you to easily change, update, re-prioritize and add detail as necessary. I use a vertical outline format in a word processor. Some people use project management software or a Gantt chart approach. Others use a spreadsheet with a horizontal format. The important thing is to use the program and format that works best for you. Whatever you do, keep it simple! Complexity and perfectionism will only bog you down and sap your motivation. (If you don't have access to a computer at this moment, don't let that stop you. Take advantage of the momentum you have right now and start your Successability Blueprint on the following blank pages.)

Before beginning, you may want to review the three sample motivation plans in the Bonus Section at the back of the book. Seeing these examples will give you a clearer picture of what your Successability Blueprint might include.

Step 1: Break the Vision Down into Manageable Goals

At the top, write down your Vision. Then brainstorm a list of goals – all the things you need to accomplish in order for your Vision to become reality. As you write them down, leave enough space between them to write down the tasks you will develop in Step 3. Try to make each goal as clear as possible.

Step 2: Prioritize Your Goals

Prioritize your goals by numbering them 1, 2, 3, etc. (On the computer, reorder the goals according to priority.)

Step 3: Break Each Goal into Tasks and Subtasks

Divide each goal into tasks. Starting with your highest priority goal, brainstorm and write down all the tasks you can think of. Then go back and find the ones that need to be divided into subtasks and write those subtasks down.

Step 4: Create a Timeline

This process may help:
- Write a start date next to your Vision. Hopefully the start date is very soon. Don't procrastinate!
- Write a start date next to the highest priority goal.
- Write a target completion date next to each task for that goal. You can add a start date to each task if you like, but if you have a lot of tasks on your Blueprint, this can become cumbersome. Some tasks will need to be finished before you start others. Plan this out as you create your timeline.
- Based on the completion date for the last task, determine a completion date for that goal.
- Repeat steps 2 through 4 for the other goals.

Based on the completion date for the last goal, determine a completion date for your Vision and write it down.

Step 5: Take Action

Highlight the three tasks that are the highest priority and begin working on those. As you complete each task, cross through it on your printed copy and later enter the strike-through on the computer file. Then highlight the next task on the timeline so that you always have three tasks highlighted. Add the three tasks to your to-do list.

Step 6: Celebrate Your Successes

Acknowledge your successful completion of tasks and celebrate your achievement of each goal.

Your Successability Blueprint

Your Vision:

iMotivate*me*

five

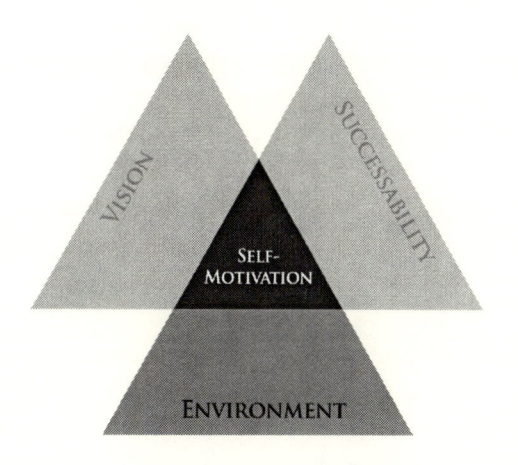

Environment

We've discussed the Vision, our worthwhile pursuit, and we've discussed Successability, our confidence in our competence. Now we are going to address the third factor in the VSE Model of Self-Motivation: Environment. When we talk about Environment as it relates to self-motivation, we are referring to not only our *Physical Environment*, that is, the place where we pursue our Vision, but also our *Social Environment*, the people and support systems we surround ourselves with.

My favorite parable is one from the Bible about a farmer who went out to the fields to sow his seeds. As he sowed, some of the seeds fell by the wayside and were eaten by birds. Some fell into the weeds, and the weeds grew up around the young sprouts and choked them out. Others fell on a rock where there was no moisture, and so the seeds withered away. Only the seeds that fell on good, fertile soil yielded strong, healthy plants.

The lesson to be learned from this parable is that our Environment has a significant influence on whether and to what degree we will succeed in our endeavors. From a self-motivation perspective, I can only be nurtured in the right Environment. If my Physical Environment detracts from my ability to manifest my Vision, I will be like the seeds that fell onto the rock and withered away. If I associate with people who have no interest in fulfilling their potential or in me fulfilling mine, I will be like the seeds that were choked out by weeds. On the other hand, if I act with intention to ensure that my Physical and Social Environments are positive and supportive, I will have planted myself in fertile soil where I can thrive and my Vision can come to fruition.

> "You are subject to your environment; therefore, select the environment that will best develop you toward your desired objective."
> - W. Clement Stone

When we operate in automatic mode, we react to our Environment without much thought. However, as intentional men and women, we can control and mold our Environment to enhance our motivation. (And even in those instances when we can't directly control our Environment, we can intentionally choose how we will respond to it.) Our objective, then, is to **manage our Environment to maximize our motivation**, and that is the focus of this chapter.

Maximize the Motivational Impact of Your Physical Environment

Physical Environment is usually what we think about when we hear the word "environment." It is a place – the space where you

Environment

do the work that is required to achieve your Vision. But it also includes the setting of that space and the objects in that space. For many people, this space will be an office, whether outside or inside their home. For others – outside salespeople, for example – it might be their car. A library could be a Physical Environment for a researcher; the gym for someone who is seeking improved health and fitness.

My Physical Environment consists primarily of an office in a spare bedroom in my home. In my office, I have a large desk and a computer. Posted above the desk are my Vision and Successability Blueprint. When I sit down at my desk, I become focused. I know I am there to work. My Environment establishes my mood, and I look forward to working on my Vision. Having a pleasant workspace leverages my motivation.

When designing your Physical Environment, if at all possible, create a place that is dedicated solely to the work of manifesting your Vision. I know that not everyone can have a place dedicated to their Vision. Your space may be the dining room table after the kids have been put to bed, and that's okay. Whatever your Physical Environment, there are strategies you can use to make it more motivating.

Strategy: **Put Yourself in a Place Where You Can Flourish**

A positive Physical Environment is one that is pleasant, encouraging and supports your work. If you enjoy being in this space, you will be more inclined to spend more time there doing the work necessary to accomplish your Vision. To create a more motivating atmosphere:

1. **Set up your Physical Environment so that you can be productive.** Gather and keep nearby equipment,

supplies, materials and resources you will need to pursue your Vision. If you work best in a neat, orderly space, keeping your Physical Environment picked up and organized is a must. If your Vision is to eat healthier, your kitchen would be a huge part of your Physical Environment. You could make it more productive by using quality food preparation equipment (such as knives, a food processor, etc.) and keeping it easily accessible.

In my workspace, everything is set up so I can work most efficiently and effectively. I have high-speed Internet for instant access to research. I also have a 19-inch wide-screen monitor that allows me to have two documents open at the same time, side by side. This makes the constant editing I have to do so much easier. I have a bookshelf next to my desk on which I keep the books related to my Vision. They are right at hand whenever I need to look up something. My Physical Environment, both the place and the things in it, make me more productive and thereby increase my motivation.

2. Set up your Physical Environment so that it is inspiring.
Posters are a great way to make your Physical Environment motivating. Many different inspirational posters are available online or at most malls. But inspiration can come from something as simple as a magazine advertisement. Above my desk I have an ad for an investment company. It's a picture of a large home, early in the morning, with a luxury car backing out of the driveway. The caption reads, "There's blind luck, dumb luck, and then there's get-up-every-morning-at-5:30-and-sweat-the-details luck."

When I first saw that ad, it had a big impact on me. I tore it out of the magazine and taped it above my computer. It motivates

Environment

me every time I look at it – not because I particularly want a big house or a luxury car, but because it reminds me that whatever it is I want, I need to work hard to get it.

Strategy: Minimize Distractions in Your Physical Environment

We all have distractions in our Environment. For me, the television has always been the major distraction. If someone in my family is watching TV and I walk into the room, I can almost guarantee that I will start watching, too. (Arguably, this is also part of my Social Environment since I enjoy spending time with my family.) But even if no one is home, it's all too easy for me to watch TV instead of doing what I need to do.

Knowing this, I had to get creative about minimizing the TV distraction. For several years, only my daughter and I lived in the house. When she turned 16 and got her own car, I told her that if she thought we didn't need cable, I would disconnect it and give her the money for gas. The cable was disconnected the next day. Without cable, the only channel my antenna picked up was the Golf Channel. Not being a big golf fan, I didn't have to worry about spending too much time watching that. I made big progress toward my Vision during that time.

When I got remarried, the problem arose again. My wife loved TV and had a job, so my offer of gas money was not particularly appealing. But when she decided she wanted a bigger home, the only condition I insisted on was that the TV be put somewhere that it wouldn't distract me from working on my Vision. We put it in a room on the other end of the house. I couldn't hear it when I was working in my office, and when I went from my office to the kitchen to get a snack, I didn't have to pass by it.

For many people, e-mails, text messages and tweets are a huge distraction. Every time you stop working to check your messages, you lose your train of thought and have to start all over again. Not only does this negatively impact your productivity, but in the end it also drains your motivation. Here's a quick solution to electronic interruptions: **Turn off the sound notification on your e-mail and phone and put your phone in another room.** I realize this may sound drastic, but is there truly anything so urgent that it can't wait an hour while you give focused time and attention to this important change you want to make in your life?

Whatever your distractions, find a way to either eliminate them altogether or minimize them as much as possible. To me, it was worth going without TV for a period of time until I achieved some of the goals I'd set. It all comes down to how strong your desire is to achieve the Vision.

Strategy: Use "Vision Reminders"

Integrating your Vision into your Physical Environment is a powerful motivator. It will keep you focused on the "why" – why you are working so hard, why you are expending your energy, why you are temporarily giving up other endeavors.

Anything that represents your Vision, that change you want to make in your life, will work. The most obvious method is to get a picture or image that represents your Vision and post it in your workspace. It could be a photo you've taken or a picture cut from a magazine or downloaded from the Internet. If your Vision is to lose weight, you could use a photo of yourself when you were slim and healthy.

You could type up your Vision statement or affirmation, print it on parchment paper and frame it, giving it the power and

Environment

prestige it deserves. Your vision reminder could also be an object. On a shelf in my work area, I keep trophies and medals from speech contests I've won, as well as my Distinguished Toastmaster medallion. All these are representations of my Vision as a professional speaker.

Motivate *me*

Maximize the motivational impact of your *Physical Environment*:

❖ What can you do to make your workspace more productive?

_____
_____

❖ What can you do to make it more inspiring?

_____
_____

❖ List all the elements in your Physical Environment that might distract you from working toward your Vision. Next to each one, list at least one thing you can do to minimize that distraction.

_____
_____

❖ Find something visual that represents your Vision and place it in your Environment.

_____
_____

Maximize the Motivational Impact of Your Social Environment

Social Environment refers to the people, support systems and organizations that surround you or are available to you. Like your Physical Environment, your Social Environment either enhances or detracts from your motivation.

The most significant part of your Social Environment is the people you come in contact with and the interactions you have with them. This includes family, friends, co-workers, colleagues, role models, mentors, peer partners, counselors, teachers and trainers.

Support systems such as professional associations, networking groups, clubs and support groups are another key element of your Social Environment. A large part of my Social Environment is Toastmasters, an organization that provides me with experience, training, mentorship and camaraderie.

> "I have seen that in any great undertaking it is not enough for a man to depend simply upon himself."
> - Lone Man of the Teton Sioux

By their very nature, Social Environments are continually in flux. I recently contracted with Wendy Kurtz of Elizabeth Charles & Associates, LLC. She is a marketing expert and publicist, but she is also a source of encouragement. Wendy is a new part of my Social Environment, one that definitely enhances my motivation.

Napoleon Hill wrote, "We begin to see, therefore, the importance of selecting our environment with the greatest of care, because environment is the mental feeding ground out of which the food that goes into our minds is extracted." As I interpret this quote, he is telling us that our Environment is where we get our beliefs,

Environment

thoughts and attitudes ... all the things that feed our mind. If, for example, we surround ourselves with people who put us down or tell us our Vision is impossible, we will be feeding our mind with negative messages. So we want to choose our Social Environment carefully. We want to surround ourselves with encouraging people, people who think we are special. We want to seek out people who will help us grow and joyfully support our pursuit of the Vision.

Your Social Environment is going to feed your mind, whether the food is healthy or not. Be intentional and make sure it is nourishing. Use the following strategies to create a positive Social Environment:

Strategy: Enlist the Support of Positive Family Members and Friends

The biggest part of your Social Environment is likely your family and friends. It's a fact of life that some of those people will be supportive and some will not. To increase your motivation, surround yourself with people who support you and limit your time with those who do not.

Some people are of the opinion that you should not share your dreams and goals with others, as they might respond with all sorts of negative messages. I believe it's worth the risk to share your Vision. It has been my experience that most people are encouraging. You may be surprised at how supportive your family and friends are. Imagine what you will gain by having them in your "corner," encouraging you daily. And you never know - someone you share your Vision with might be in a position to help you. You might even find a mentor.

Of course, there is always the possibility that someone will be negative or condescending or belittle your Vision. (If so, you might want to consider finding different friends.) If you know in advance that certain family members or friends are toxic (unhealthy for you) because of how they have behaved in the past, don't share your Vision with them, limit your time around them and look elsewhere for support.

Strategy: Find a Peer Partner

Having a companion on this journey to manifest your Vision will make it much more pleasant, so find yourself a peer partner. A peer partner is someone who will be there to nudge you when you get distracted, reassure you when you are discouraged, and be a sounding board when you don't know which way to go. Your peer partner may be a friend, colleague or someone you meet at a support group.

Two of my friends are peer partners for each other. Neither was taking action toward her Vision until they began coaching each other. They have found that two heads are indeed better than one and that having a support system makes the process easier and more fun.

Be intentional when choosing your peer partner. Find someone who will help you rather than impede you. Don't consider someone who you know can't or won't be there for you or someone who will doubt you or try to dissuade you. Your significant other can be your peer partner, although someone who is not so close to you can often fill the role better. We often don't accept feedback from our significant other as well as we do from other people.

When you decide on someone, approach them and ask them to be your peer partner. Be clear about what you are asking them to do and explain why you have chosen them for this role. Your peer partner doesn't need to have the same Vision as you; in fact, they don't even need to have a Vision. But if they do, you could offer to be their peer partner in return.

Strategy: Join a Support Group

No matter your Vision, there likely exists a support group full of people with the same desire as you. A support group can be a professional association, a club, an organization like Weight Watchers or an informal group of like-minded individuals (like the other members of your exercise class at the health club). A support group will encourage you, keep you on track and help keep you accountable. And it can provide you with many additional benefits, such as networking opportunities, access to more experienced people, instruction and training, a feeling of belonging, and a safe place to try out and practice new behaviors.

As I mentioned earlier, my primary support group is Toastmasters. I belong to two Toastmaster clubs; one is a regular club and the other is for professional speakers. Twice a week I am involved with a group of people who believe that growing as a public speaker is important.

If your Vision is to run a marathon, search Google for a local running club. If your dream is to write a book, find a writers' group in your area. There is a support group for just about every conceivable Vision. It may not be as precise a fit as Toastmasters is for me, but there will be one that meets your need for support.

Strategy: Find a Mentor

A mentor is an experienced and trusted counselor and coach. A mentor agrees to actively support and encourage you, and more importantly, to serve as a guide on your path to your Vision. Having a mentor as part of your Social Environment is a very powerful way to positively impact your motivation.

I'm often asked about the difference between a mentor and a peer partner. First, in a mentoring relationship, the support, wisdom and advice flow from the mentor to you, the mentee. In a peer relationship, the flow of support, wisdom and advice is two-way, between you and the peer. The second difference is that a mentor has already achieved success in the area your Vision relates to, while a peer partner is typically "at the same level" as you. If your Vision is to become an executive chef, your mentor would likely be an executive chef of a successful restaurant, while your peer partner might be a fellow student at culinary school.

Where do you find a mentor? Sometimes he or she will just appear, as in, "When the student is ready, the teacher will appear." But if not, it is perfectly appropriate for you to seek a mentor. There are many resources for finding a mentor. Your support group is an excellent place to look. Consider a former professor, someone you used to work for or an acquaintance who has already achieved success. If your Vision is to start a business, the Small Business Administration offers several mentoring programs. One such program, SCORE (Service Corps of Retired Executives), works with individuals to help them start and grow successful businesses.

Finally, consider being a mentor for someone else. You have plenty of wisdom and advice to share. Helping others achieve their Vision can be a powerful boost to your own Successability.

Motivate *me*

Maximize the motivational impact of your *Social Environment*:

❖ Write down at least one family member or friend who you believe will support you in achieving your Vision.

❖ Think about and write down at least one person whom you would consider asking to be your peer partner.

❖ If you already belong to a support group, write the name of that group below. If not, research and write down the names of support groups related to your Vision.

❖ Write down your mentor's name or the name of someone whom you would like to be your mentor.

In order to maximize your Environment, both physical and social, you must do two things. First, you need to identify the things and people in your Environment that inhibit your motivation and eliminate or at least minimize them. Second, identify the things you can do within your Environment to increase your motivation ... and then do them!

You are well on your way to manifesting your Vision. Unfortunately, the reality is that there will be challenges along the way, things that will stop your motivation cold. I call these roadblocks "detractors." We will learn about detractors and how you can overcome them in the next section.

SUMMARY

- With respect to self-motivation, Environment has two aspects:
    - Physical Environment – the place where you pursue your Vision
    - Social Environment – the people and support systems you surround yourself with

- You can control and mold your Environment to enhance your motivation.

- Strategies to maximize the motivational impact of your Physical Environment:
    - Put yourself in a place where you can flourish
    - Minimize distractions
    - Use "vision reminders"

- Strategies to maximize the motivational impact of your Social Environment:
    - Enlist the support of positive family members and friends
    - Find a peer partner
    - Join a support group
    - Seek a mentor

Part II

STRATEGIES TO INCREASE YOUR MOTIVATION

iMotivate*me*

six

Detractors

We now understand the Self-Motivation Model and that influencing any of the three factors – Vision, Successability and Environment – will likewise influence our motivation. Up to this point, we've focused on strategies to increase our motivation by positively impacting the three factors. In this chapter, we will look at situations that negatively impact our motivation, what I call *detractors*, and more importantly, strategies to overcome them.

In self-motivation, we use the word "detractor" in the broadest of terms. Anything that reduces your motivation or keeps you from working toward your Vision is a detractor. Detractors can affect any or all of the three factors.

> **Detractor**
> Anything that reduces your motivation or keeps you from working toward your Vision.

As with the other aspects of self-motivation, detractors are unique to each individual. Some detractors will have absolutely no power over you, while others will be forces for you to reckon with. The goal, of course, is to eliminate detractors, or at least minimize their impact, so that we remove any barriers that stand in the way of our success. The popular saying, "Knowledge is power," attributed to Sir Francis Bacon, is very true when it comes to self-motivation. When we become aware of our personal detractors, we can take steps to overcome them. For every detractor, there is a strategy to counteract and nullify its power.

Let's examine the most common detractors. As you read, actively reflect on the information and ask yourself, "Is this a detractor in my life?"

Naysayers

A naysayer is a person with an aggressively negative attitude. Nothing is ever right with naysayers, and they don't mind telling you what is wrong with your ideas, hopes and dreams. Naysayers feel threatened by you pursuing your Vision, and the things they say are a reflection of their own fears, jealousy and lack of motivation. Sadly, we all know people like this.

Naysayers will rob you of your motivation if you let them. They can damage your self-esteem and cause you to doubt the choices you've made. Most often, their challenges will be directed at your Vision. But they can also make you question your Successability, your ability to achieve the Vision.

Mark Twain said, "Keep away from people who try to belittle your ambitions." That's good advice, and we've talked at length about creating a positive Social Environment. But the reality is that we can't always isolate ourselves from negative co-workers or naysayers who are otherwise loving family members. When confronted with naysayers, remember that their negativity is the result of their own emotional baggage. In actuality, it has nothing to do with you or your Vision. Don't buy into their garbage and let it distract you from your worthwhile pursuit. Don't let them define you or convince you to settle for less.

Strategy: Turn a Naysayer into a Positive Motivational Force

When you can't avoid naysayers, use their words as a motivating challenge to fuel you to work even harder. I recall several years ago when I mentioned to a fellow lawyer that I was working on my Master's in Education. His comment was, in effect, "That's your goal today. What are you going to come up with tomorrow?" Then there was the friend who said to me, "Bob, you'll never leave the security of your present job to become a speaker. No way."

Rather than let these comments gnaw at me, zap my motivation and make me doubt myself and my Vision, I considered them a challenge. I immediately made a small poster, writing on it only, "The Challenge" and taped it over my desk (my Physical Environment). Every day when I sat down to work, I looked at that poster and thought about those naysayers and what they had said. And it motivated me ... a lot!

Turn a negative into a positive. Use naysayers and their criticisms to drive you harder and faster. Turn their "You'll never do it" into "Want to bet? Just watch me!"

The #1 Naysayer

So what do you do if the biggest naysayer in your Environment is *you*? I have a lot of experience with this, as I am usually my harshest critic. I ask myself, "Why would anyone want to hear what I have to say about motivation?" or I tell myself, "You never follow up on what you start." Self-deprecating talk, in which you continually spout negative things about yourself, is clearly de-motivating.

Psychologists can help us understand why we are so critical of ourselves – that topic alone could fill an entire book. Suffice it to say that many of us are hard on ourselves, harder than we would ever be on someone else. (By the way, there's nothing wrong with acknowledging your mistakes. Just remember, criticize the mistake rather than yourself for making it.)

If you are like me and you are the most negative person in your Social Environment, there is bad news and good news. The bad news is that unlike other naysayers whom you can choose not to associate with, you are, of course, with yourself 24/7. There is no escaping the full-time critic that is you. Whenever you need some good old criticism, you are always there to provide it!

But here's the good news: You are in control. You may not be able to make your father stop telling you that you'll never amount to anything or make your friend stop joking about your inability to maintain a relationship, but you have total control over what you say to yourself. Granted, it may be difficult to get *you* under control, but one thing is for sure: You have more control over yourself than you have over anyone else.

The Golden Rule says, "Do unto others as you would have them do unto you." The corollary to that is, "Don't do to yourself what you would not do to others." You wouldn't say such negative things to anyone else; don't do it to yourself!

Strategy: Become Your #1 Cheerleader

How do you stop being your own worst critic? Here are a few simple tips to becoming your own best cheerleader:

- ❖ Whenever you catch yourself being critical, stop and take a deep breath. Examine your self-criticism. Nine times out of ten, you'll find it is overly harsh or even unwarranted.

- ❖ Revisit your Stories of Achievement (page 36).

- ❖ Every evening before you fall asleep, acknowledge what you accomplished that day.

- ❖ Give yourself continuous, positive verbal feedback or "pats on the back." By engaging in positive self-talk, you will defeat the naysayer and increase your motivation.

Fear

Fear wreaks havoc on our motivation. As long as we are afraid, we will not be motivated to pursue our dreams. Fear is like instinct in that it serves the purpose of alerting us to possible danger. But in today's world in which we are rarely faced with life-threatening danger, we often direct our fear toward perceived rather than actual threats.

When it comes to the Vision, the two things we tend to fear the most are: 1) the enormity of the change we want to make, and

2) not knowing what the change will involve. In other words, we perceive that the risk of pursuing our dream is too great. This creates doubt and insecurity. We lose our confidence and then we lose our motivation.

Most of us view fear as a negative. But in her wonderful book, *How Not to Be Afraid of Your Own Life*, Susan Piver writes, "Fear heralds a boundary reached." Looked at this way, the feeling of fear tells you that you are getting ready for a courageous new step.

My favorite quote about fear is from Ambrose Hollingworth Redmoon. Redmoon spent the last three decades of his life in a wheelchair after a car accident left him a paraplegic. Redmoon said: "Courage is not the absence of fear, but rather the judgment that something else is more important than one's fear. The timid presume it is lack of fear that allows the brave to act when the timid do not. But to take action when one is not afraid is easy. To refrain when afraid is also easy. To take action regardless of fear is bravery."

Redmoon's point is this: Don't let fear rule you. As humans who are uniquely capable of reflection, we have the power to rationally look at our fears and decide what action we want to take. We must be intentional. We must decide whether we are going to let our fears be bigger than our Vision. If that is our choice, at the very least we've made a conscious choice.

Strategy: Leverage Your Courage

What do we do if we just aren't very brave? If we look deep down within ourselves, we will see that there is in fact courage there. Maybe not a lot - probably not as much as we would like - but it is there. Look within yourself and acknowledge your courage and the brave things you've done. Some possibilities might include:

- ❖ Doing what was right even though it was unpopular or cost you money;
- ❖ Standing up for yourself or someone else;
- ❖ Standing up for a principle or idea;
- ❖ Taking a big risk;
- ❖ A time when you kept going even though you felt sure you would fail and it would have been easy to give up.

Remembering times when we were courageous allows us to leverage the courage we do have. When we couple that courage with the clarity and control that we achieve with a Successability Blueprint, we can tackle just about anything. We break our Vision into a series of steps that we are brave enough to take. For example, let's presume our Vision is to start our own company, to be our own boss. This is pretty scary stuff, even for a brave person. But when we break it down into smaller steps, each step seems less risky, less frightening and more doable:

1. Determine what kind of business we want to start (not too scary and maybe lots of fun).
2. Research our prospective business (lots of work, but still not risky).
3. Put together a business plan (even more work, perhaps creates some fear, but doable).
4. Make an outline and a timeline of the steps we need to take to implement the business plan (transforms something we perceive as very risky and frightening into something less so).
5. Start implementing the business plan, one step at a time (we can leverage our courage to take each step as it comes).

By breaking that major change into its component parts, we can eliminate some fear and leverage our courage to overcome any remaining fear. You can use this strategy anytime you doubt your ability to accomplish a task or project. If you will break it down, you will see that it's not so risky or scary after all.

Distractions

Perhaps the most common detractor is distractions. Distractions are anything that temporarily seduces you away from pursuing your Vision, goals or tasks. You may refer to them as temptations, time wasters or delay tactics. Distractions have strong motivating power. Unfortunately, it is the power to motivate you to *ignore* the work you need to do to manifest your Vision.

Distractions typically confront us with the choice of immediate versus long-term gratification, that is, the immediate gratification of the distraction versus the long-term gratification of achieving the Vision. We are most susceptible to them when we're doing something that isn't particularly interesting or fun. Distractions can be exciting situations (a friend who calls with tickets to the game tonight), though they are just as likely to involve passivity on our part (mindlessly surfing the web).

Distractions can be deceiving. For one thing, they are temporary and typically don't knock you completely off course. (For example, "Just for tonight I'll watch TV, and tomorrow night I'll get back on my life-changing work.") But don't be fooled by them. Yes, they are temporary, but they are insidious and pervasive. If you let them, they will rob you of your motivation and keep you from achieving your Vision, one day at a time.

They are also deceiving because they appear to be unimportant yet they can easily derail us. Everyone's heard the saying, "Don't sweat the small stuff." But we need to sweat the small stuff when it comes to our motivation. Distractions that seem small often have a very powerful and negative impact on our motivation.

As I've already mentioned, my number one distraction is the television, as it is for many people. As long as I pay the cable bill, I'll have at my command hundreds of channels, all waiting to entice me. Instead of writing a blog entry, it's all too easy to sit down in front of the television and watch a mixed martial arts match or flip over to a movie channel to see which action movie is on. And it doesn't matter if I've seen it before – I'll watch it again!

If you don't already know what they are, it's important to look carefully at your life and identify your distractions. When you examine them, you will likely find they are part of your automatic self. They are your unthinking, habitual activities, such as checking e-mail every 15 minutes, immediately reading incoming text messages, answering the phone or chatting mindlessly with a talkative friend. Remember, there is no law that says you must answer the phone when it rings.

Once you become aware of your distractions, they are usually not too difficult to overcome. When you find that you have been seduced by your distraction, think about what was going on before you succumbed. Notice it and write it down. When you have been tempted but successfully avoided the temptation, write that down, too, noting how you avoided it and what you told yourself to get back on track.

The real challenge is that distractions must *continually* be overcome because they are typically ever-present. Fighting distractions is an ongoing war rather than a one-time battle. Fortunately, losing a battle occasionally will not keep you from achieving your Vision. But that's the key – making sure the distractions only win occasionally.

Distractions are such a threat to your motivation that I'll offer three strategies to defeat them:

Strategy: **Get Rid of the Distraction**

The first strategy is to get rid of the distraction if you can. The television distraction got so bad for me that I put it on semi-permanent hold when I turned off my cable. If you have a family, getting rid of the TV or cable may not go over well. (If that's the case, try the next strategy: Turn Your Distractions into Motivators.)

With other temptations, however, this strategy works great. I have a friend whose Vision involves losing weight and being healthier. At a recent meeting at a local restaurant, I noticed that she asked the waitress not to bring any bread to the table. She knew the smell of that freshly baked bread would just be too much for her level of motivation and that she wouldn't be able to resist. So she simply eliminated the temptation.

You can use this strategy with junk food, too. If you're like me, when you're at the grocery store, you tell yourself you'll get something as a "treat" and eat it only once a week. Yeah, right! For most of us, if the ice cream, potato chips or soda are at home, we'll eat them – every day. It's a lot easier to not buy them at all than to buy them and try to resist them.

If the phone is a major distraction, put it on silent mode or forward your calls. Are you addicted to checking e-mail, texts, tweets and Facebook? Set a schedule and stick to it. For example, "After one hour of solid work on my Vision, I will check e-mail." Managing your distractions is all about being intentional with respect to the stimuli in your life.

Detractors

Strategy: Turn Distractions into Motivators

With this strategy, we turn distractions into motivators by using them as a reward. All that is necessary is to practice delayed gratification. Although most experts say external motivation does not have as much impact as internal motivation, many people find that giving themselves rewards for successful completion of tasks or goals increases their motivation.

Delayed gratification is learning how to balance short-term and long-term pleasure. It involves making an intentional choice rather than automatically doing that which gives us pleasure right now. Being able to delay gratification is frequently necessary if we are to succeed in making our dreams come true.

Think about the events and situations that distract you. Oftentimes, you will discover that they involve your desire for short-term satisfaction to the detriment of your long-term goals. It's human nature to want pleasure today. But we also need to understand that giving up a lesser pleasure today will result in a greater pleasure tomorrow (in my case, foregoing watching yet another action movie for being a published author and sought-after speaker). When you internalize the idea that *not* getting the short-term desire will likely improve your life in the long term, the temptation will not be as great.

If you are a TV junkie like me but can't get rid of your TV, use it as a reward. Record your favorite shows. Then promise yourself that if you work on your Vision for two nights, you will spend the third night watching TV. If your major distraction is video or computer games, you can do the same thing. Work hard for an hour or two; then reward yourself with playing Xbox for 30 minutes. Just be sure you set a timer!

Strategy: Set Parameters for Distractions that Can't or Shouldn't be Avoided

Some distractions are unavoidable and rightly so. For example, you may have a family. This can certainly be a distraction, an unquestionably important distraction, but a distraction nonetheless.

With situations such as this, the best strategy is to set boundaries or parameters. For instance, explain to your children that you will read a book, play one game or play baseball with them for 20 minutes, and then you have to do some work. After you do an hour's work, you can play again. Or make an agreement with your spouse that you will each work on your respective Visions at the same time each day, without interrupting each other, and then do something together.

Another option for distractions that shouldn't be avoided is to find a way to incorporate them into your work toward your Vision. If your Vision is to live a healthier lifestyle, have your children ride their bicycle with you while you run or take your spouse with you to the gym. (This adds some accountability as well!) Or, if it doesn't create too much of a distraction, share your Physical Environment with your spouse. While you work toward your Master's degree, he or she works on the photography business, both of you in one room together.

You have to assess the situation and set the boundaries or parameters you think are appropriate for the situation. A 2-year-old requires hands-on time, but a 5- or 6-year-old can play by him/herself for a certain period of time. The important thing is to make intentional decisions and not just operate in automatic mode.

Motivate *me*

What are the three most powerful distractions in your life? Write down each one, as well as at least one strategy for overcoming it.

Distraction	Strategy
1. _____	_____
2. _____	_____
3. _____	_____

The Blame Game

The blame game is what happens when we look outside ourselves for the causes of our problems. In the blame game, we blame circumstances or other people or both. Here are some things you might find yourself saying if you are playing the blame game:

The other person didn't do what he/she was supposed to do.

It's the economy.

It's my genetics.

My car wouldn't start, so I couldn't....

I don't have enough time to....

I don't have enough money to....

I couldn't get my computer to work.

My dog ate my homework!

We play the blame game in order to excuse ourselves and avoid responsibility for our perceived shortcomings. One of the problems with the blame game is that you spend time *excusing* mistakes that would be better spent *correcting* them. The bigger problem is that when you blame other people or the situation, you are admitting that you are not in control. This means you are giving up your power, which reduces your Successability and your motivation.

Strategy: Eliminate Excuses

> The fact that *sometimes* there may be *some* validity to the finger-pointing of the blame game doesn't make finger-pointing any more effective. The solution is simple: Be aware; be intentional. When you find yourself playing the blame game, pause and ask yourself, "**If I couldn't use that excuse, what would I be doing differently?**" Then go ahead and do it.

Complaining

I was reading *The Science of Getting Rich* by Wallace D. Wattles recently when I had an epiphany. I was already familiar with affirmations – the science behind them, how much power they have and how to create them. But what I'd never realized until reading Wattles' book was that **complaining is a negative affirmation**. This notion is so simple; yet think of the enormity of it. It made me wish I'd spent as much time on my positive affirmations as I had on my negative affirmations (my complaining).

Every time we complain about something or someone, we are affirming the truth of that complaint. For example, if I complain about how relationships rob me of my freedom, I am affirming that any relationship I get into will do just that. This negative affirmation would program my subconscious mind to look for women who are demanding and controlling. And if you're at all like me, you don't just complain about something once – you tend to repeat it, frequently! Every time you do so, you are programming your subconscious mind with negativity – the very stuff that you are unhappily complaining about – and inviting even more of it into your life. We all need to quit!

Strategy: Use a Visual or Kinesthetic Reminder

How did I quit my complaining? I'd be lying if I said I've quit completely, but I have drastically reduced the frequency. And sometimes that's as good as one can do. Negative affirmations are often very ingrained in us, so we need a constant visual or kinesthetic reminder to stop and catch ourselves when we are in the midst of complaining.

My visual reminder – and one that many people use – is a bracelet. Think about it ... your wrists are with you 24/7, everywhere you go. And since they're connected to your hands, you tend to see them frequently. The silicone bracelets that are popular now are great reminders. You can get them with different inscriptions or just plain. But any bracelet (or even a thick rubber band) will work. I settled on an attractive metal bracelet. It's loose, and as it wanders up and down my arm, it serves as a reminder to stop my complaining. It has worked wonders.

Many people also use a kinesthetic reminder such as wearing their watch on the other wrist or a ring on a different finger. Because it feels unnatural, it serves as a constant reminder.

Frustration

It's almost a given that you're going to experience some frustration on the way to achieving your Vision. People will make promises that they won't keep. Deadlines that you've established will come and go, unmet. Computers will crash. People you must interact with will be crabby or even rude. In fact, if you're not getting frustrated, at least occasionally, you're probably either exceedingly lucky or you aren't aiming high enough with your Vision.

There's nothing wrong with being frustrated. It's a perfectly normal response when things don't go the way we'd planned. The problem arises when our frustration becomes so great or long lasting that it de-motivates us to the point that we stop working toward the Vision.

Our ability to handle frustration is called *frustration tolerance*. Studies have shown that people have different levels of frustration tolerance. When confronted with a difficult task, someone with low frustration tolerance will lose his/her temper, break down in tears, become aggressive, look for someone to blame or just give up. A person with high frustration tolerance, on the other hand, persists when faced with a challenge, even though the task is difficult and the situation isn't going his/her way. Those with high frustration tolerance can weather disagreement and opposition and are better able to maintain their motivation.

Strategy: Train Yourself to Increase Your Frustration Tolerance

Fortunately, you can increase your tolerance for frustration and therefore your ability to maintain your motivation in the face of challenges. The first step is to learn to accept frustration. Acceptance is the key. As the Buddhists point out, we would prefer to not have frustration in our lives, but if it happens, we know it won't kill us. We may experience disappointment, we may experience annoyance, and that's okay.

Then, learn to "play" with frustration by intentionally putting yourself in situations in which you are likely to become frustrated. Give yourself permission to experience the feeling and then move on. Tell yourself, "This is not the way I want this situation to be, but it is tolerable. I can live with this situation the way it is." The purpose of this exercise is to internalize the reality that frustration may be uncomfortable and inconvenient but that "this too shall pass."

The Feeling of Having Failed

It is an incredible experience when you achieve your goals and conquer your "mountains," but life doesn't always turn out that way. What if you grab for the brass ring and it slips out of your hand? The journey to your Vision may not always be a smooth one. There will be missteps, roadblocks and dead ends. There will be struggles and outright failures. Sometimes your best just won't be good enough. Perhaps you don't get called back after the second-round job interview, or you lose 20 hard-fought pounds only to fall off the wagon and gain it all back.

It's pretty obvious that failure negatively impacts motivation. However, it is not failure that causes the problem, but rather our response to it. This is why I say the detractor is the *feeling of having failed* rather than failure itself. Failure hurts, and when you operate in automatic mode, your instinctive reaction is to avoid pain. Failure affects the decisions you make and can make you gun-shy about taking risks.

I used to be a prosecutor. I experienced several failures – they were called defense verdicts. When I lost a case, I felt like I never wanted to try another case again. However, it was my job, my income. Quitting wasn't an option, so I'd get back up on the horse and try another one.

But when you are your own boss going after your Vision, it's all too easy to quit and give up. I believe Napoleon Hill had it right when he said, "Before success comes in any man's life, he's sure to meet with much temporary defeat and, perhaps, some failures. When defeat overtakes a man, the easiest and the most logical thing to do is to quit. That's exactly what the majority of men do."

Failure is unpleasant, there is no denying it. But failure, by itself, will not defeat you. As long as you get up again, you will be undefeated. Oliver Goldsmith, an 18th-century Anglo-Irish poet wrote, "Our greatest glory is not in never falling, but in rising every time we fall." Yet the reality is that for most of us, it's difficult to get back up when we've experienced a setback. Here is a great strategy that intentional people use to keep failure from robbing them of their motivation:

Strategy: Capitalize on Your Failures

Every mistake or failure is merely an unwanted result, an opportunity for learning. This is the positive aspect of what we call failure.

Naval ships in World War II had amazingly big guns that fired shells at targets on land. When the gunner thought he was on target, he would fire the gun. He observed where the shell landed and modified his aim accordingly. If the shell landed to the left of the target, he moved the gun to the right. If it fell short of the target, he raised the gun. The gunner didn't bemoan the fact that he missed the target and think of himself as a failure. He simply corrected for the error. Each time he did so, he got closer to the target. He only had to hit it once to be successful.

You can choose to see failure as nothing more than an unwanted result and use it to fine-tune and correct your actions. Every mistake has a cause, which you can discover and change to produce a different result. Thank failure for the lessons it can teach you and use it to get closer to your target.

Perhaps you weren't as prepared as you should have been for that job interview. Decide that you'll be on top of the situation next time and write down what you'll do differently. Maybe you gained weight because you stopped using those exercise DVDs. Perhaps the learning is that you need to join a gym where you will have a support group and be more accountable for going.

As Ken Christian says in *Your Own Worst Enemy: Breaking the Habit of Adult Underachievement*, "Those who do not milk failure for what they can learn from it squander a major opportunity." Don't let your mistakes and failures defeat you. Instead, learn from them and adjust accordingly. Then pick yourself up, dust yourself off and start all over again.

SUMMARY

A detractor is anything that reduces your motivation or keeps you from working toward your Vision. Detractors can negatively impact any or all three factors of self-motivation. Common detractors and strategies for overcoming them include:

- **Naysayers** – people who are negative toward you or your Vision.
  Strategy: Turn naysayers and their negativity into a positive motivational force by seeing the situation as a challenge.

- **The #1 Naysayer** – *you!*
  Strategy: Become your #1 cheerleader by constantly using positive self-talk.

- **Fear** – when you perceive that the risks of pursuing your dream are too great.
  Strategy: Remember past courageous acts and leverage the courage you already have.

- **Distractions** – temptations, time wasters or delay tactics that temporarily pull you away from pursuing your Vision, goals or tasks.
  Strategy: Get rid of the distraction.
  Strategy: Turn distractions into motivators.
  Strategy: Set boundaries or parameters for distractions that can't/shouldn't be avoided.

- **The Blame Game** – blaming circumstances or other people for your problems.
  Strategy: Eliminate excuses by asking, "If I couldn't use that excuse, what would I do differently?"

- **Complaining** – a negative affirmation that is reinforced every time you repeat it.
  Strategy: Use a visual or kinesthetic reminder to catch and stop yourself when you complain.

- **Frustration** – you will likely face difficulties on the way to achieving your Vision.
  Strategy: Train yourself to increase your frustration tolerance.

- **The Feeling of Having Failed** – it is not failure that causes problems, but rather your response to it.
  Strategy: Capitalize on your failures by seeing every mistake or failure as an unwanted result and an opportunity for learning.

Motivate *me*

Identify and write down your three biggest detractors. They could be detractors discussed in this chapter or something unique to you. Next to each one, write down what you will do to neutralize or lessen its impact on your motivation – either a strategy discussed in this chapter or a strategy of your own.

Detractor   **Strategy**

1. _____   _____

2. _____   _____

3. _____   _____

iMotivate*me*

seven

Enhancers

Sometimes we're just not motivated to do the work necessary to achieve our Vision. You'd think we'd be motivated all the time. After all, the Vision is something that is worthwhile, a change that we truly desire in our lives. So why aren't we motivated to make it happen? Darned if I know! Even after studying and writing about self-motivation for so long, I still find myself unmotivated at times.

But you know what I've discovered? It doesn't matter why we're not motivated. What matters is *what we do about it*. Now when I'm unmotivated, I'm usually able to catch myself more quickly than I used to. And when I do, I take proactive steps to increase my motivation and quickly pull myself out of that space.

There are several strategies I use for getting out of a state of low motivation. I call these strategies *enhancers*. Just as detractors decrease your motivation, enhancers increase your motivation. And like

> **Enhancer**
> Anything that increases your motivation or supports you in your quest to manifest your Vision.

detractors, enhancers are unique to each individual.

Enhancers impact several or all of the three factors of Self-Motivation (Vision, Successability, Environment), and for that reason, they are super-strategies that will turbocharge your motivation. Let's take a look at my favorites.

Revisit Your Vision

When you are feeling flat out unmotivated and need to get moving again, reconnect with your Vision. Ideally, your Vision is posted somewhere in your Physical Environment. Read it out loud to yourself. Envision what your life will be like when you have manifested that Vision and make the image in your mind as real as possible. Try to get in touch with how you will feel when you have reached that point. Reflect on what you've accomplished on your journey so far. When you revisit your Vision, you reconnect to all the motivation your Vision has to offer.

Reconnecting with your Vision is crucial when faced with tasks or activities that are not intrinsically motivating. The reality is that some of the tasks we must accomplish in order to achieve our Vision are not much fun. In fact, some might be downright drudgery. But success is often built on drudgery. If we don't complete the tasks, the goals won't be met. If the goals aren't met, the Vision will not come to fruition. If some of the tasks are a grind, we just need to grind them out.

But it's how we go about grinding out those tasks that makes the difference and determines how motivated we will or will not be.

When we say we *have* to do something, we are verbally giving up our power. We are like a child who is being forced to put away his or her toys. The child probably isn't going to do a good job, and he or she will be an unpleasant bugger the whole time.

But we, as adults, have a choice. In these situations we can choose to say, "I'm not particularly enjoying what I'm doing right now. This is not giving me pleasure, but I *want* to do it because I know it is in my best interest to do it." Maybe "it" involves giving up something in the short term, because we know in the long term it will pay off. Maybe "it" involves doing something healthy instead of something unhealthy.

Does this shift in attitude really make a difference? I think it does. When we truthfully say, "This is what I *choose* to do," we are exercising our power — our power over our circumstances and our power over our pleasure-seeking self. Exercising our power is motivating. *Wanting to* is motivating. *Choosing to* is motivating. *Having to* is not motivating.

The next time you're faced with some task that is drudgery but you know is in your best interests and you find yourself thinking, "I hate having to do this," stop yourself. Reconnect with and focus on your Vision; remind yourself why you are doing this particular piece of drudgery; accept that you are doing *exactly what you want to be doing*; and say out loud, "I want to do this." Once you accept that you are truly doing what you *want* to be doing and that you are doing it freely, the resentment you are feeling will fade away and be replaced by motivation and determination.

Leverage Your Motivation

Motivational Leveraging™ is one of the most powerful enhancers I am aware of. In financial terms, leverage is the ability of a small investment to produce a large return. We can use a similar concept with self-motivation, that is, leverage what motivation we do have into even more motivation and get more bang for our buck, so to speak.

I first became aware of the potential power of this concept years ago, before I even started studying motivation, when I heard the story of the brownie and the mayonnaise from a man who was giving a talk on weight loss. He shared that when he traveled, he struggled to maintain his diet. Back then, the airlines served a light meal. As soon as he would open the package, he was confronted by the dessert, usually a brownie or a cookie.

Now this man knew that he could resist the brownie while he still had the sandwich to eat, but that once he finished the sandwich, the temptation of the brownie would be too strong and he would succumb. His motivation to stay on his diet would not be strong enough to resist the brownie as it sat in front of him until the flight attendant came by to pick up the trash. Knowing this, the first thing he would do when he got his meal was open up the little package of mayonnaise that came with the sandwich and spread the mayo all over the brownie. Once he'd done that, the brownie no longer tempted him.

This man understood that his motivation to eat healthy and get slim was not as strong as it needed to be in that situation. So he was intentional and leveraged what motivation he did have into even greater motivation. By acting quickly, before the call of the brownie became overpowering, he was able to stay on his diet. This gentleman didn't call it Motivational Leveraging, that's my phrase, but this was the first time I became conscious of this powerful concept.

With Motivational Leveraging, when your motivation just isn't strong enough to accomplish a certain task or activity, you do an intermediate task for which you *do* have enough motivation, and that intermediate task accomplishes the bigger objective.

As a personal example, one of my major distractions is movies. But I am intentional; I know this about myself. I know that if I have a DVD at home, it will tempt me all night and frequently wear me down. The key for me is "at home." To tempt me, the DVD must be at my house. Once I'm at home without a DVD, it's too much hassle to go back out and rent one. But when I drive home, I pass right by a video rental store. That is when temptation strikes, and The Sirens begin calling to me. Do I stop or keep going? My motivation is not strong enough to resist a DVD in my house, but it is strong enough to keep my foot on the accelerator as I speed by the video store. It only takes 15 seconds of resolve to keep going, and I can stay motivated for those 15 seconds by thinking about my Vision.

I can leverage a quarter of a minute of self-control into two hours of work. That's what Motivational Leveraging is all about: Giving our limited motivation much greater impact. If I were to stop and rent a DVD, it is possible (although improbable) that I could avoid the temptation of watching it. The result would be the same – two hours of work toward my Vision – but not getting the DVD in the first place takes a lot less motivation.

A great way to use Motivational Leveraging is with coaches and trainers. Many people use a personal trainer to assist them with an exercise program. They know they don't have enough motivation to go to the gym and work out for an hour on their own, but they do have enough motivation to get to the gym twice a week if they have an appointment with a trainer. Once there, a trainer encourages them to keep working and pushes them to improve. The limited amount of motivation they have, strategically leveraged, produces far greater results. The exact same Motivational Leveraging concept works with group exercise classes. You may not have enough motivation to work out on your own, but you will go to a class that meets at a certain time each week and let the instructor motivate you.

If a gym membership isn't in your budget, you can still leverage your motivation with a peer partner. Find a neighbor or friend who also wants to get in better shape and commit to walking or jogging together every Monday, Wednesday and Friday morning. You will likely have enough motivation to make the arrangement with your partner. After all, it will be healthy for you, and you won't have to actually walk until some later date. When that day comes, however, and the shoes have to hit the road, the thought that it is healthy for you may not be enough to get you up and going. But you made a commitment to your partner who is going to be waiting for you at the end of the street. Making that initial commitment takes just a little motivation, and once you've committed, you are more likely to follow through.

There are lots of ways you can leverage your motivation. By being creative, being intentional and taking charge of your motivation, you, too, can become a motivation powerhouse.

Develop Good Habits

We've talked a great deal about the importance of being intentional. So it may seem paradoxical that one of the best ways to increase your motivation is by developing good habits. A habit is an action or behavior that is regularly followed until it becomes *automatic.*

The Divide and Conquer strategy showed us that we need to break down our Vision into goals and our goals into tasks. Some of our tasks will be one-time actions, while others will be repetitive tasks that need to be done continuously. For example, if one of my goals is to get physically fit, a one-time task might be to join a gym. A repetitive task would be to go to the gym every Monday, Wednesday and Friday. Making habits out of these repetitive tasks is one of the best ways to guarantee we will successfully manifest our Vision.

We can also develop good habits for other self-motivational activities that *should be* repetitive or continuous, such as minimizing distractions, not complaining, checking in with a mentor or peer partner, engaging in positive self-talk or repeating affirmations.

Creating a new habit is not complicated. Research indicates that to form a habit we simply need to repeat the action for 21 days in a row. When I decided to make saying affirmations a habit, I quickly found out that it's easier said than done to repeat an action for 21 straight days. Although it seems easy to create bad habits, doing a good thing repetitively is, for some reason, a bit more difficult. Here are some tips for turning important repetitive tasks into productive habits:

- ❖ **Write down the habit you want to create.** The clearer you are about exactly what you want to do every day, the more likely you are to do it.

- ❖ **Get clear about *why* you want to make this behavior into a habit.** What are the benefits of the habit? The more important it is to you, the more likely you are to do it every day.

- ❖ **Do the behavior at the same time every day.** You probably shower and brush your teeth about the same time every day. These are habits you've developed. Likewise, you will increase your chances of creating a new habit if you repeat the desired behavior at the same time and in the same place every day. (I decided to repeat my affirmations first thing in the morning when I sit down at my desk, even before I read my e-mails.)

- ❖ **Start small.** This is especially helpful if you want to get in the habit of saving money. If you are like most people, you don't think you make enough money to save anything. So just save a little amount, something that won't hurt very much. Once you're in the habit of saving, every time you get a raise, bonus or cash gift, you are much more likely to take a portion of that money and put it into savings.

- ❖ **Enlist the help of your Social Environment.** Depending on the habit you want to establish, figure out how you can get others to help hold you accountable to repeat the behavior for 21 days. For example, if you want to make a habit of taking a walk every evening after dinner, consider asking your spouse to help you reach the required number.

- ❖ **Keep track of your progress.** Writing it down forces you to be intentional. You can keep a journal, cross off days on a calendar or use an electronic tracker such as the Google Gadget "Don't Break the Chain" or iPhone app "Streaks." Every day that you complete your action or behavior, mark it on the calendar. Once you have a streak going, you will be motivated to keep it going.

Make a Promise

Here's a typical evening for me: I know I need to write and publish a blog. But I also need to answer some e-mails and watch a video on increasing blog readership. *Well,* I think, *I can do those two things tomorrow night.* But then I remember that I meet with my mastermind group that night, so it will be Friday before I can get those things done. But I know I shouldn't wait until Friday. Maybe I should just forget it all and watch TV and start fresh bright and early Saturday morning....

Does this sound familiar? You go back and forth, trying to decide which priority is the highest or whether you should work or "play." Before you know it, your indecisiveness has robbed you of any motivation you might have had, and the call of your distraction becomes overwhelming.

One evening when I was faced with this situation, something snapped. I made a decision. And I made a promise. I said to myself, "I promise I will not watch a movie/DVD tonight. I will answer e-mails and write my blog." A load was immediately lifted from my mind. There was no more going back and forth about what I would do. Prior to making the decision, I was weighing the choices, and the choices were pretty much in balance. But once I made the commitment, it was as if an additional weight had been added to the scale, a weight that made the choice clear.

I am amazed at the power of simply deciding to commit. Once you make a promise, there is no going back. It's all you need to do to bring the matter to a close. And making a promise to someone else is just as powerful as making a promise to yourself. This is one reason why having a peer partner can be so helpful in staying motivated. A peer partner is someone you make a promise to, and a promise has power.

I urge you to try this strategy the next time you are weighing choices, especially when you know exactly what the right choice is. By the way, have you noticed that many of the self-motivational strategies – such as getting a peer partner, having a mentor, leveraging your motivation and making a promise – are connected or overlap? These strategies are so powerful because they employ multiple motivational techniques.

Be Open to Inspiration and Life-Changing Opportunities

Inspiration literally means the spirit within. It can come from anywhere and manifest itself in many ways: A great idea comes to you from out of the blue. An acquaintance makes a remark in passing that triggers your imagination and creativity. You're flipping through a magazine in the doctor's waiting room when you "by chance" see an article that pertains to your Vision.

The spirit can strike at any time – sitting in your car in traffic, during your workout, while taking a shower. My particular time is 3:30 – *A.M.* – when I should be asleep, when I need to be asleep because I have to get up in four hours to go to work. But that's when it comes. In the past when inspiration struck at that time, I'd say, "Yeah, that's a good idea; I'll have to use that." Then I'd roll over and go back to sleep.

The next evening I'd sit down at my computer and ... nothing. I couldn't remember what the great idea was. I'd rejected a gift. I'd said, "No thanks. I'd rather roll over and go back to sleep." After leaving too many of these gifts on the table, I now take notice. When inspiration comes, I get up, turn on the light, get the pad of paper I leave on my nightstand and start writing.

As you get serious about manifesting your Vision, you will spend more and more time working toward it, and more and more of your energy will be directed toward it. Your brain will be thinking about it even when you are focused on other things. When your inspiration comes, whenever and wherever that might be, *listen and take note!*

The same is true with life-changing opportunities. They present themselves to us frequently, but we often don't recognize them.

Sometimes these opportunities are dramatic – getting laid off from a job makes possible the opportunity to start the business you've always dreamed about. Other times they are just little hints of what could be. So keep your eyes and your heart open to the possibilities. And when you see an opportunity, take it! Major life *changes* do not magically occur, even though the *opportunities* to make these changes will often "magically" appear. When they do appear, we need to accept them and step through the door that has opened.

One of my affirmations is, "When I have an inspired thought, I act on it. When a door opens, I walk through it." Inspiration and opportunity are gifts – gifts from the One who gives, whomever you believe that is. Don't leave these precious gifts on the table.

Identify Your Unique Motivators

You know better than anyone else what motivates you. While I was working on this book, my brother moved to town and brought his 1200 Harley Davidson Sportster. Though I hadn't ridden a motorcycle since I was in my 20s, after riding his, I took the motorcycle safety foundation course and decided to get my own.

But rather than rushing out and buying one, I made the decision to make it a motivator. I committed to not buy one until I'd written and published this book. I pinned a picture of the motorcycle I want to buy above my desk (in my Physical Environment), and it gives me one more reason to spend time in the evenings working toward my goal. It's working! When the book is published, I will have my bike.

You, too, will find things in your life that can serve as motivators. It can be something big that you want to purchase or something small, such as going to a movie after you write out your Vision.

The important thing with this strategy, as in everything else in self-motivation, is to be intentional. Be the one to pull your own strings.

SUMMARY

Enhancers increase your motivation and keep you working toward your Vision. Enhancers can positively impact any or all three factors of self-motivation.

- ❖ **Revisit your vision** – envision what your life will be like when you have manifested that Vision; make that image as real as possible in your mind.

- ❖ **Leverage your motivation** – when your motivation isn't strong enough to accomplish a certain task or activity, do an intermediate task for which you *do* have enough motivation, and that intermediate task will accomplish the bigger objective.

- ❖ **Develop good habits** – repeat actions or behaviors for 21 days in a row to create a habit for repetitive tasks, minimizing distractions, not complaining, checking in with a mentor or peer partner, engaging in positive self-talk or repeating affirmations.

- ❖ **Make a promise** – commit to yourself or to someone else to do the right thing to move you closer to your Vision.

- ❖ **Be open to inspiration and opportunities** – pay attention, take note and take action when inspiration and opportunity find you.

- ❖ **Identify your unique motivators** – what drives your motivation more than anything else?

Motivate *me*

Identify and write down two to three strategies you can use to enhance your motivation. They could be enhancers discussed in this chapter or something unique to you.

1. _____

2. _____

3. _____

iMotivate*me*

Part III

PUTTING IT ALL TOGETHER

**iMotivate*me*

eight

Create Your Unique Motivation Plan

I like to surf the Internet to see what other people are writing about self-motivation. I often read articles and blogs that offer "helpful hints," "rules" or "suggestions," the purpose of which is to help you become motivated. I would never deny that these are good ideas. My concern is that they don't come together into a comprehensive and cohesive program for becoming and remaining motivated.

In order to become motivated and stay motivated, you need a plan. Haphazard attempts at getting yourself motivated are not going to work. If you're like me, there are too many things going on in your life to expect motivation to just happen. Only by having a plan will you be able to keep yourself motivated. The VSE Model for Self-Motivation provides a framework to create your motivation plan.

The other problem I have with motivational tips offered by others is that they are generic – they don't take into account individual differences. The ability to develop a *customized* plan is what makes

> "He who fails to plan, plans to fail."
> - Proverb

the VSE Model for Self-Motivation different and more effective. Rather than being a series of behaviors that are designed to motivate the "average" person, the VSE model presents a practical way for you to determine what motivates *you*.

It takes a little more work to design an individualized motivation plan than to read a series of hints, but aren't your dreams worth it? Aren't they worth spending some time to make a plan?

I hope you answered "yes" to those questions because we are now ready to bring together everything you've learned so far and create your unique motivation plan. This customized plan will encompass the specific strategies that work for you and apply to your situation. It will take just a little time to put together, but once completed, it will show you exactly what you need to do to get and stay motivated.

An effective motivation plan includes:

- ❖ The Checklist – a tool for identifying the elements of your plan
- ❖ The Successability Blueprint – a step-by-step path to reach your Vision
- ❖ The Motivation Map™ – a visual representation of your plan that will keep you motivated long enough to work the Successability Blueprint

Before you begin creating your unique motivation plan, I recommend you review the three sample motivation plans in the Bonus Section at the back of the book. Seeing these examples will give you a clearer picture of what your finished plan might look like and include.

The Checklist

Over the course of this book, I've shared many strategies for increasing your motivation. Those strategies are recapped on the checklist on the following page. (This checklist can also be downloaded for free from my website, www.iMotivateMeTheBook.com.)

Take a few minutes right now to go through the list and put a check mark next to the strategies you think will work to help you enhance your motivation to achieve your Vision. It doesn't matter how many or which ones you pick. Choose the ones that resonate with you.

MOTIVATION PLAN CHECKLIST

Strategies to maximize the motivational power of the Vision:
- ❏ Focus on the "whys"
- ❏ Do a cost analysis
- ❏ Replace rather than eliminate
- ❏ Write your Vision as an affirmation and visualize it every day

Strategies to increase your Successability:
- ❏ Know your strengths
- ❏ Examine your self-imposed limitations and self-fulfilling prophecies
- ❏ Discover your stories of achievement
- ❏ Focus on what you can control
- ❏ Enhance your abilities
- ❏ Create success experiences
- ❏ **Divide and Conquer super strategy – create your own unique Successability Blueprint**

Strategies to maximize the motivational impact of your *Physical Environment*:
- ❏ Set up your Physical Environment so that you can be productive
- ❏ Set up your Physical Environment so that it is inspiring
- ❏ Minimize distractions
- ❏ Use "vision reminders"

Strategies to maximize the motivational impact of your *Social Environment*:
- ❏ Enlist positive family and friends in your journey
- ❏ Find a peer partner

- ❏ Join a support group
- ❏ Find a mentor

Strategies for overcoming detractors:

- ❏ Turn naysayers and their negativity into a positive motivational force by seeing the situation as a challenge
- ❏ Become your #1 cheerleader by constantly using positive self-talk
- ❏ Remember past courageous acts and leverage the courage you already have
- ❏ Eliminate excuses by asking, "If I couldn't use that excuse, what would I do differently?"
- ❏ Use a visual or kinesthetic reminder to catch and stop yourself when you complain
- ❏ Train yourself to increase your frustration tolerance
- ❏ Capitalize on perceived failures by seeing each as an unwanted result and an opportunity for learning

Strategies for dealing with distractions:

- ❏ Eliminate or minimize the distraction
- ❏ Turn your distractions into motivators
- ❏ Set boundaries or parameters for distractions that can't/shouldn't be avoided

Strategies for enhancing your motivation:

- ❏ Revisit your vision
- ❏ Leverage your motivation
- ❏ Develop good habits
- ❏ Make a promise
- ❏ Be open to inspiration and opportunities
- ❏ Identify your unique motivators

The Successability Blueprint

Although there might be Visions for which the path to achieving them is so clear that a Successability Blueprint is not necessary, those will be few and far between. As I mentioned earlier, the Divide and Conquer concept is what I call a super strategy. If I could tell you only one thing that would give you the best chance of manifesting your Vision, it would be to create a Successability Blueprint because it clearly and concisely lays out the path, step by step, to your Vision.

If you did not create a Successablity Blueprint in Chapter 4 or check off the Divide and Conquer strategy on the Checklist, I encourage you to reconsider using this strategy. Even if your Blueprint is nothing more than a handful of goals, it will still provide you with some crucial direction and milestones. If you did check off the Divide and Conquer strategy on the Checklist but have not yet created your Successability Blueprint, go back to Chapter 4 and do that now.

The Motivation Map™

Now that you've identified the elements of your self-motivation plan, we're going to use a tool called a Motivation Map to capture the plan. I developed Motivation Mapping based on concept mapping – a technique for visualizing the relationships among different concepts. The Motivation Map is a visual representation of your motivation plan. It helps you stay in an intentional state by keeping you aware of all the things in your life that impact your motivation.

A Motivation Map will help you in four ways:

1. It forces you to write the plan down, so that you have clarity. Clarity is motivating.
2. You will be able to see the connections between the various elements of self-motivation.

3. It provides a constant reminder of what you need to do to become and stay motivated.

4. It continues to stimulate your mind as you review it on a daily basis, so that you can continually fine-tune your motivation plan.

While Motivation Mapping can be done on a big sheet of paper, most people prefer to create their Motivation Map on a computer using a spreadsheet, specialized software like Inspiration or any of the myriad of flow-chart programs that are available. You will be continually reviewing your Motivation Map, tweaking it so that it will better guide you and fit your path. This need to update the Map is why using a computer is easier. On my website (www.iMotivateMeTheBook.com) is a downloadable spreadsheet with a generic Motivation Map. I recommend you use this Motivation Map to get started. Simply open the spreadsheet and replace the generic terms with words appropriate for your Vision and plan. On the following page is an example of a generic Motivation Map:

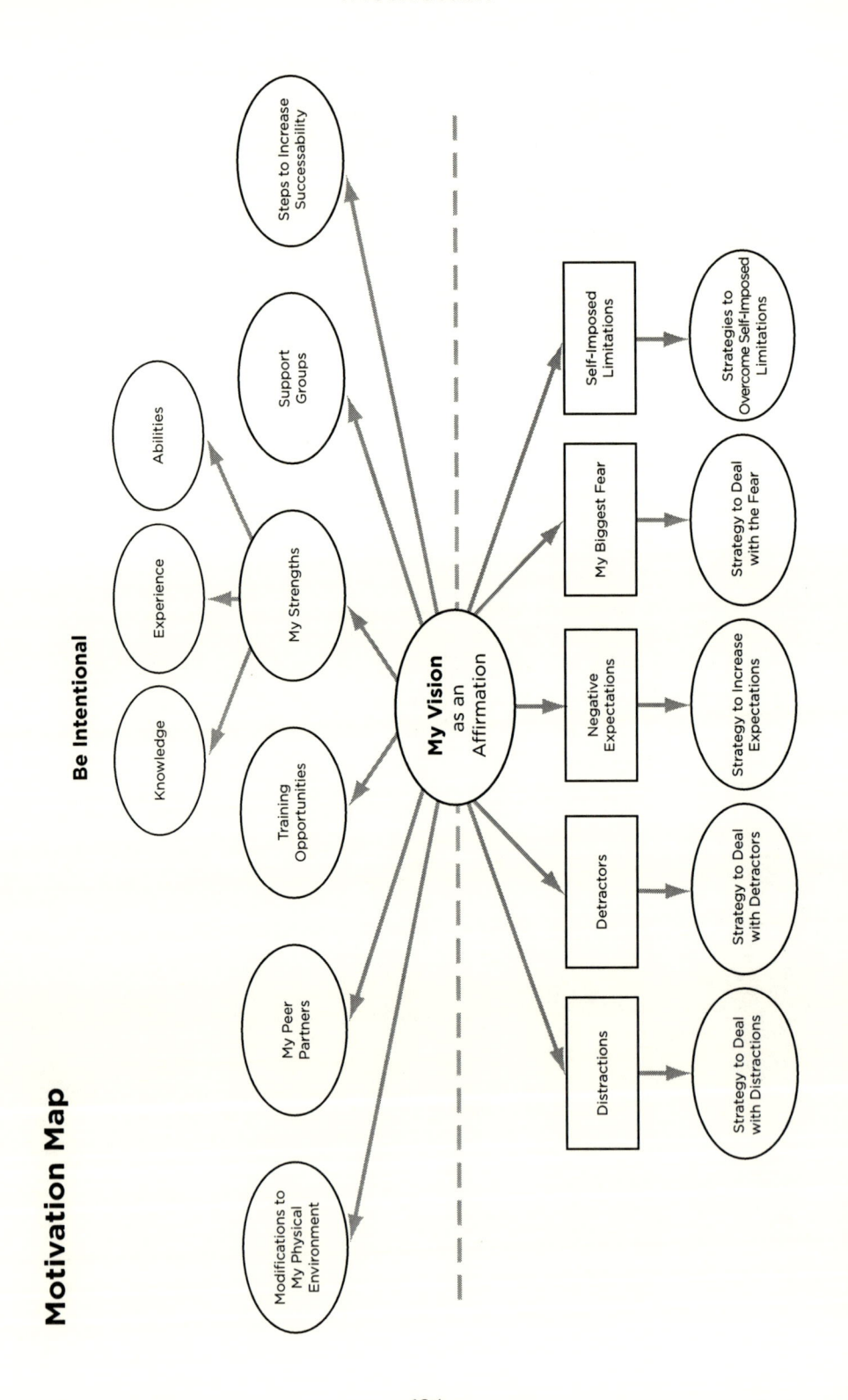

*i*Motivate*me*

Motivation Map

Be Intentional

- Steps to Increase Successability
- Support Groups
- Abilities
- Experience
- Knowledge
- My Strengths
- Training Opportunities
- My Peer Partners
- Modifications to My Physical Environment

My Vision as an Affirmation

- Self-Imposed Limitations → Strategies to Overcome Self-Imposed Limitations
- My Biggest Fear → Strategy to Deal with the Fear
- Negative Expectations → Strategy to Increase Expectations
- Detractors → Strategy to Deal with Detractors
- Distractions → Strategy to Deal with Distractions

Create Your Unique Motivation Plan

To make your Motivation Map, you will need the answers to the questions and exercises you've completed throughout this book and the list of strategies you chose on the Checklist. Then follow these steps:

1. Place a circle in the middle of the page and write your Vision in it. (Note: You will have a different Motivation Map for each Vision.) For greater motivation, write your Vision as a positive affirmation.

2. Write the words "Be Intentional" at the center top of your map to remind you to stay in an intentional state.

3. Draw a horizontal dotted line through the Vision circle.

4. On the upper half of the chart, above the line, you will write down things that increase your motivation. These are the things you want to focus on and do more of. Start by drawing an oval for each strategy or enhancer you checked on the Checklist — those positive, motivating things that support you on your path to your Vision. Inside the oval, write a few keywords or a phrase to represent the item. Be sure to include at least one or two strategies that will increase your Successability and at least one or two ways to create a positive Environment. Things that go above the line might include:

    ❖ Reasons why your Vision is so important to you
    ❖ Opportunity costs of not achieving the Vision
    ❖ Your strengths, special talents and positive attributes that will help you manifest the Vision
    ❖ Aspects of the Vision that you have control over
    ❖ Your stories of achievement
    ❖ Brave, courageous things you've done

- ❖ Success experiences
- ❖ Modifications to your Physical Environment to increase your motivation
- ❖ Names of family and friends who will support you and your Vision
- ❖ Name(s) of your peer partner(s)
- ❖ Name(s) of your support group(s)
- ❖ Name of your mentor
- ❖ Distractions that you can turn into motivators
- ❖ Good habits you will develop
- ❖ Skills and abilities you will enhance
- ❖ Training opportunities
- ❖ Your unique motivators

5. On the bottom half of the chart, below the line, you will write down the things that decrease your motivation. These are the things you want to avoid or minimize. Draw a rectangle for each detractor – the negative, de-motivating things that hold you back or block you from achieving your Vision. Inside the rectangle, write a few keywords or a phrase to represent the item. Things that go below the line might include:

- ❖ Self-imposed limitations
- ❖ Negative expectations and self-limiting beliefs
- ❖ Negative self-fulfilling prophecies
- ❖ Your biggest fear
- ❖ Distractions in your Physical Environment
- ❖ Temptations, time wasters or delaying tactics
- ❖ Names of naysayers in your life
- ❖ The word "ME" if you are your #1 naysayer

- ❖ Complaints you frequently repeat
- ❖ Frustrations
- ❖ Any negative response (such as anger) to feeling that you have failed

6. Under each rectangle that represents a detractor, draw an oval and connect it to the rectangle above. In the oval, write a few keywords that represent a strategy you will use to counteract the detractor.

Work the Plan

Now the only thing left to do is to work your plan. The Successability Blueprint is the step-by-step path that will lead you to your Vision. The Motivation Map is the customized plan that will keep you motivated long enough to work the Successability Blueprint. Post both of them in your Physical Environment where you can look at them every day. Start implementing your plan immediately by adding the first three tasks from the Successability Blueprint to your weekly to-do list.

Your motivation plan will guide you to a new you. If you follow it faithfully, you will achieve your Vision – the worthwhile pursuit or change you want to see in your life.

SUMMARY

❖ In order to become motivated and stay motivated, you need a customized plan.

❖ The VSE Model for Self-Motivation provides the framework to create your motivation plan. An effective motivation plan includes:

✦ The Checklist – a tool for identifying the elements of your plan

✦ The Successability Blueprint – a step-by-step path to reach your Vision

✦ The Motivation Map – a visual representation of your plan that will keep you motivated long enough to work the Successability Blueprint

nine

Continuous Improvement

You've created your customized motivation plan, and hopefully, you've begun implementing it. Now you need to ensure it will continue to work and that you can adjust it as necessary as you gain experience and wisdom about yourself. The way to guarantee this ongoing improvement is through evaluation.

When I think about evaluation, I think of the words from the Kenny Rogers song "The Gambler": "You got to know when to hold'em, know when to fold 'em, know when to walk away, know when to run." When things aren't going well and you don't seem to be making progress toward your Vision, you need to be open to the possibility that you've made a wrong turn somewhere. Assessing your plan – and how well you're following it – allows you to recognize your mistakes, learn from them and make the necessary course corrections to get back on track toward achieving your Vision.

> "Feedback, that is, how you are doing, is an essential part of motivation."
> - Fran Tarkenton

And what if things are going great? Do you still need to evaluate? Absolutely. Knowing what *is* working is often more beneficial than understanding what *isn't* working. Furthermore, the satisfaction and positive reinforcement of knowing you are on track has the motivational power to propel you forward even faster.

When Should You Evaluate?

There are two ways to time your evaluations, and you'll want to use both:

❖ **On a regularly scheduled basis**

Evaluating your progress at regular intervals forces you to be systematic and intentional in looking at what is truly going on. At these evaluations, review your efforts over the previous period to assess what you've achieved and then take time to appreciate your accomplishments.

To determine a schedule that will work best for you, think about your Vision and your motivation plan. For most situations, a weekly checkup is effective. It gives you enough time to make some progress, yet doesn't allow enough time for negative patterns to develop. I do a regular evaluation once a week, but I also do a mini-evaluation every day. At night as I lay in bed, before I drift off to sleep, I review what I did that day to further my Vision.

❖ **On an as-needed basis**

In addition to your regularly scheduled evaluations, you'll also want to stop and assess the situation when something positive happens and when something not-so-positive happens.

When you achieve favorable results or after you've taken a big step toward your Vision, you want to look at what worked so you can duplicate the same process and achieve even better results next time. Do your evaluation immediately after the positive event happens and praise yourself for your courage, for taking a risk or for the results of your hard work. Giving positive feedback immediately after a positive result is *motivating* feedback. This is a time for celebration, so make sure you bask in the feelings of satisfaction and success.

When you hit a dead end, make a mistake, discover that you aren't moving forward or start doubting yourself, you also want to understand why. But in this case, it's so you can take steps to keep it from happening again. In these evaluations, you analyze the results, identify what you could have done better, and plan your next step. After less-than-desirable results, consider giving yourself a little time (perhaps a few days) before doing the evaluation. This will often give you valuable hindsight and needed perspective. It also provides some emotional distance from the event, which is important if you were disappointed, frustrated or angry that things didn't go according to plan.

How Do You Evaluate?

When you do an evaluation, you are essentially looking at your plan, or what was expected, and comparing it to what you actually accomplished. As with any self-assessment, first and foremost, you must be honest with yourself. Denying the truth only reduces your chances of achieving the Vision. You want to celebrate your successes, but you also need to get gut-wrenchingly honest and look for places where improvements can be made.

That said, evaluation should enhance your motivation, not detract from it. Without too much thought, it's easy to see how an evaluation could turn into a de-motivating experience. To prevent that from happening, we use what I call the Drucker Ratio.

Peter Drucker was arguably one of the most influential thinkers and writers in business management. He posited that people generally perform well four times as much as they perform inadequately. Therefore, managers should praise workers four times as often as they criticize, correct or otherwise speak negatively to them. The ratio of positive feedback to negative feedback, Drucker argued, should be the same as the ratio of good work to inadequate work. Have you ever worked for a manager who followed the Drucker Ratio? Bosses like that are not very common.

Fortunately, we control the type of manager we are to ourselves and the type of feedback we give ourselves. We want to foster high Successability, encourage ourselves and increase our motivation. We do that by maintaining the Drucker Ratio when we evaluate our work toward the Vision:

$$\frac{\text{Good work}}{\text{Inadequate work}} = \frac{4}{1} = \frac{\text{Praise}}{\text{Criticism}}$$

It's a simple concept, but so many of us are far more likely to criticize rather than praise ourselves. So here are four steps to follow in your evaluations that will help you maintain the Drucker Ratio:

1. Give plenty of self-praise.
   At each evaluation, recognize your forward movement, even if slight, and acknowledge your attempts, even if they weren't

completely successful. When you give positive reinforcement, you encourage the same behavior in the future.

When praising yourself, follow the same rules that management and parenting experts offer for praising other people:

- ❖ Be precise in your praise, specifying exactly the behavior you want to repeat (clarity is motivating)

- ❖ Emphasize the behavior (to reinforce more of the same)

- ❖ Praise soon after the event (to increase the motivating power)

2. Identify any Gaps

A Gap is the difference between what you planned to happen and what actually did happen. With the clarity afforded you by the Successability Blueprint and the Motivation Map, comparing the "plan" to "actual" is easy. Look at what you expected to happen – that is, what you wrote down on your Successability Blueprint and Motivation Map – and compare it to what occurred. Any discrepancy is the Gap.

Again, this is when self-honesty is crucial. Overcome any inclination you may feel to deny that a Gap exists or to rationalize *why* a Gap exists. Keep in mind that setbacks and relapses are a normal part of progress, and above all, don't beat yourself up.

In order to resolve them, it's important to identify any Gaps as precisely as possible. Here are some questions that should be helpful:

- ❖ Are you completing your tasks? If not, that is the Gap.

- ❖ Are you accomplishing your goals? If you aren't, that is your Gap.

❖ If you are accomplishing your tasks and your goals but your Vision is not coming to fruition, that is the Gap.

❖ Are you missing skills or abilities that are necessary to achieve your Vision? Those are Gaps.

❖ If you set a goal to get some training to enhance those missing skills but you haven't completed it, that is a Gap.

❖ If you have identified your distractions but have not implemented strategies to eliminate or minimize them, that is a Gap.

If there are no Gaps – that is, you are on target with your Successability Blueprint and Motivation Map and everything is progressing smoothly – look for places where you can improve or accelerate your progress.

3. **Determine how to bridge the Gap**

Once you have identified any Gap(s), you must discover *why* there is a Gap and figure out what actions are necessary in order to close it. Bridging the Gap is not about dumping on yourself. It's about learning from your mistakes and looking for solutions. Everyone makes mistakes, but just because you've made a mistake doesn't mean you've learned something from it. Learning means knowing how to perform differently the next time.

When you are looking to bridge any Gaps, the focus should be on the future, not the past. Instead of asking why something went wrong, ask how you can make it work the next time. The focus should also be on correcting the behavior rather than "fixing" you. *You* are just fine. It's your actions or your behaviors that need to change. Your goal is to stop non-productive behavior (in my case, succumbing to distractions) but not stop yourself. Concentrate on specific behaviors or actions you've taken or not taken, rather than on you as a person, and avoid labeling, characterizing or defining motives.

The purpose of bridging the Gap is to come up with solutions that are well defined (clear) and achievable (motivational) in order to get you back onto the path to manifesting your Vision. Here are some thoughts to consider:

❖ How do you feel about your Vision? Is it still motivating you? Do you need to restate it?

❖ If you are completing your tasks but the goals aren't being met, or you are completing your goals but not manifesting your Vision, you've probably misidentified the tasks/goals. The solution is to establish new, different tasks/goals that will definitively lead to your Vision.

❖ If you *aren't* completing your tasks/goals, you need to figure out why.

✦ Are they unclear? If so, restate them more clearly.

✦ Are they too difficult? Do you have unrealistic expectations? If so, you need to redefine them and then set new, reasonable tasks/goals.

✦ Are there obstacles that are preventing you from completing them? If so, you need to figure out how to overcome these obstacles.

✦ Do you need to boost your Successability? Are you perhaps missing some needed skills? If so, what type of training can you get to develop those skills?

❖ Are there changes to your Environment, either physical or social, that will help you bridge the Gap? When my evaluations showed that I wasn't accomplishing my plan, almost invariably my Environment was causing the Gap.

❖ Are there detractors or distractions getting in the way? Examine them; are they temporary or chronic?

4. **Make adjustments to keep your Blueprint and Map current**
As you pursue your Vision, "life" will happen. New detractors and new distractions will appear. Your Environment may change. Sometimes, as you work your plan, you will uncover new information that necessitates changing or adding to your plans. As I worked to manifest my Vision, I learned that having an effective visual presentation was a key component of a powerful speech. As a result, I had to add another goal to my Successability Blueprint: develop a solid visual component.

I have a friend whose Vision was to start his own business. He researched various franchise opportunities and eventually settled on one. But as he delved deeper into the process, he came to the conclusion that it wasn't a good fit for him after all. He didn't give up on his Vision, thank goodness. He simply had to change his Successability Blueprint and motivation plan with respect to what kind of business he would pursue.

Evaluations provide the opportunity to step back, take stock of where you are, identify what has changed since you created your plan and determine what, if anything, needs to be tweaked.

On page 139 is a template to guide you through your evaluations. You can also download this form for free from my website, www.iMotivateMeTheBook.com and modify it to suit your needs.

At the beginning of this book, I talked about the importance of being able to motivate yourself 24/7. That is the sure path to achieving your Vision. To stay motivated, you must constantly be evaluating and revising your plan to ensure it stays current. Make your Successability Blueprint and Motivation Map living documents, a testimony to your life that will continue to evolve.

SUMMARY

❖ Periodically evaluating and assessing your motivation plan allows you to celebrate your achievements as well as recognize your mistakes, learn from them and make the necessary course corrections to get back on track toward achieving your Vision.

❖ Evaluate your progress on both a regularly scheduled and as-needed basis.

❖ Self-honesty is crucial in assessing your progress toward your Vision.

❖ The Drucker Ratio suggests a 4:1 ratio of positive to negative feedback.

❖ A Gap is any difference between what you planned to happen and what actually did happen.

❖ Bridging the Gap is about learning from your mistakes, looking for solutions and focusing on the future.

❖ To evaluate your progress:

- ✦ Give plenty of self-praise
- ✦ Identify any Gaps
- ✦ Determine how to bridge any Gap(s)
- ✦ Make adjustments to keep your Blueprint and Map current

Motivate *me*

1. How often do you think you should do your regularly scheduled evaluation?

   _____

2. Schedule your first evaluation on your calendar.

3. Use the Evaluation Guide on the following page (or download a free copy) to assess your progress at your first regularly scheduled evaluation.

MOTIVATION PLAN EVALUATION GUIDE
Remember the Drucker Ratio – 4:1 Positive to Negative Feedback

1. Give plenty of self-praise
- What tasks have you accomplished since the last evaluation?
- What goals have you achieved since the last evaluation?
- What things (specific behaviors) have you done well?
- What lessons have your successes taught you?
- What can you do even better to achieve greater success?
- How will you celebrate the work you've done toward achieving your Vision?

2. Identify any Gaps
- What did you expect to achieve since your last evaluation?
- Did you achieve it?
- How many tasks remain before each goal will be accomplished?
- How many goals remain before your Vision will be achieved?
- What things did not go as well as you would have hoped?
- Are you on schedule according to your timeline?
- Clearly and precisely identify any Gaps.

3. Determine how to bridge the Gap
- Identify the reason for each Gap.
- How can you bridge each Gap? Specifically, what will you do differently going forward?
- What lessons can your missteps teach you?

4. Make adjustments to keep your Blueprint and Map current
- Do you need to "fine-tune" your Vision?
- What goals or tasks will you focus on going forward?
- Do you need to add/change goals?
- Do you need to add/change tasks?

When will you evaluate again?

iMotivateme

Take Charge of Your Motivation

Do you ever fantasize that your Vision – the change you desire in your life – is just going to magically occur? Perhaps someone will walk into your office and offer you a fantastic new job or a great deal on an ongoing successful business. Maybe you'll win the lottery and solve all your financial challenges. Or perhaps a pill that will quickly and easily melt away the pounds without diet and exercise will finally be invented.

If you have these or similar fantasies about your Vision, you are committing the number one mistake people make that causes them to *not* achieve their dreams: wishful thinking. "Wishful thinking," my dad always told me, "will get you nowhere fast."

Positive thinking, affirmations, meditations and prayer are a wonderful way to *start* getting the things we want out of life. I do all four and highly recommend them. But they are only the start.

After the positive thinking, the affirmations, the meditations and the prayers comes the work. *You've got to do the work.* You have to take action to make the changes you want in your life.

So why do so many people get derailed or stuck on their journey to achieving their dreams? In my experience, it's not because they are lazy. I think most people are willing to do the work necessary to achieve their Vision. The problem comes in getting and staying *motivated* to do the work, and that means **motivation is the difference between merely wishing for something and actually having it.** It doesn't matter what your Vision is … without motivation you aren't going anywhere.

And yet, expecting that you will magically become motivated is also wishful thinking. Sure, there are probably people who have been motivated since birth. But I suspect most people (like me) are not naturally motivated. Nor does the motivation fairy pay them a visit each night.

If you aren't naturally motivated, face that fact and take the steps necessary to motivate yourself. There is no better motivator on the planet than the person who knows you the best – *you*. By taking charge of your motivation and creating a customized plan for your circumstances, you can overcome challenges and obstacles and become your Vision.

As you've seen throughout this book, it really is fairly easy to take charge of your own motivation. And you now have the tools to motivate yourself anytime, anywhere. If you don't use them to achieve your dreams, there's no one to blame but yourself.

On the other hand, **if you will create a motivation plan** *and follow it*, **you** *will* **achieve your dream.**

Use the VSE Model for Self-Motivation – value your Vision, increase your Successability and maximize your Environment. Go to www.iMotivateMeTheBook.com and download the free resources to help you develop your customized motivation plan, Successability Blueprint and Motivation Map. Do regular evaluations to ensure continuous improvement. As you work toward your Vision, if you lose your motivation and your momentum, come back to the book, review it again and try some different strategies.

If you have questions, don't hesitate to send me an e-mail at Bob@BobAPrentiss.com. In addition, as a reader of my book, I invite you to become part of my Social Environment. (You can find my social media information on my website, www.BobAPrentiss.com.) Let me know what you like about the book and what does and doesn't work for you. If you have success stories to share or strategies that you've found to be effective in motivating yourself, I look forward to hearing about those as well.

I truly believe you can have everything you want in life. It's just a matter of motivating yourself to do what it takes to achieve your dream. Find something you want, make the commitment to motivate yourself to stay on your path, and you *will* find what you seek.

iMotivateme

bonus

Sample Self-Motivation Plans

The VSE Model for Self-Motivation can be applied to a multitude of circumstances and situations. In this bonus section, we will look at examples of how it can be used to positively impact three common changes that people want to make in their lives regarding health and fitness, career and finances.

Health and Fitness

In Chapter 4, I introduced you to Stephanie, a woman who wanted to lose weight and get healthy. As you may recall, Stephanie's Vision written as an affirmation was: *Me Slim*. She utilized a number of Vision and Successability strategies to increase her motivation. With the Divide and Conquer strategy, she created a Successability Blueprint that clearly showed the path to her Vision through achievable goals and tasks. Now, let's look at the rest of her customized motivation plan.

The main aspect of Stephanie's Physical Environment as a stay-at-home mom was her kitchen. She maximized the motivational power of her Physical Environment by: 1) keeping it stocked with healthy, ready-to-eat foods, 2) getting rid of all the junk food, and 3) posting on the refrigerator and pantry door pictures of herself when she was slim. This served to both inspire her and remind her of her Vision when she was tempted to splurge.

The most important element of her Social Environment was her supportive husband and children who, understanding how important weight loss was for their mother, went without all the treats they loved.

Stephanie made Weight Watchers a key part of her motivation plan because it positively impacted both her Successability and Environment. Through Weight Watchers, she received training on setting appropriate weight-loss goals, nutrition, stress eating, making wise food choices and preparing healthy meals. The point system used in Weight Watchers guided her in choosing what and how much to eat, giving her both clarity and control. As a result, she gained tremendous confidence that she could manifest her Vision.

Weight Watchers is one of the biggest organizations of people for whom being overweight is or was a major issue in their lives. By joining, Stephanie immediately became part of a support group that cheered her victories, held her accountable and proved by example that she could attain her Vision. Even after losing the weight, she was able to stay in the organization as long as she maintained a healthy weight. Stephanie made a good friend at Weight Watchers and has made that friend a part of her Social Environment as well.

Social Environment was crucial for another of Stephanie's goals – to exercise regularly. She "test drove" several gyms and found that each of them had a distinct "personality." One catered to serious bodybuilders, another only to women. Eventually she found one where she felt "at home," and because she felt comfortable around the people there, she was more motivated to go. Over time, she made friends with some of her fellow gym-goers and asked one of them to be her peer partner.

To overcome her negative self-talk about her previous inabilities to lose weight and keep it off, Stephanie used positive affirmations, repeating them twice a day, morning and evening. She also committed to herself that she would view setbacks and slip-ups as learning opportunities rather than failures. Each time she went off her diet, she analyzed the root cause and discovered that she was a stress eater. That knowledge led her to learn new skills at Weight Watchers to prevent future setbacks.

Stephanie's biggest distraction with respect to her diet was junk food. Her strategy for dealing with junk food was two-fold. First, she eliminated the distraction by getting rid of all the junk food and sweets in the house. Now, as you might imagine, her family wasn't so crazy about this idea at first, but she convinced them this strategy would benefit them as well. She took the strategy one step further by using dessert as a motivator or reward. If she met her exercise and food goals for the week, on Sunday nights the entire family went for ice cream. This promise of a sweet treat motivated her to stick with her plan during the week (not to mention that it encouraged her family to support her!). And because they went *out* for dessert, the junk food was not in the house where it might tempt her. In addition, they always went someplace where she could get low-fat frozen yogurt, which she had learned at Weight Watchers was a better choice than ice cream.

Stephanie enhanced her motivation with several strategies. First, she leveraged her motivation by finding an exercise that she enjoyed. It took her a couple of tries to find one, but when she did, it made all the difference. Because she liked spin class, it required a lot less motivation to go to spin class three times a week than to work out by herself on the treadmill or stair climber.

She also made a conscious decision to make exercising a habit. By joining a gym and finding a group class she liked, she helped herself establish a good habit of exercising at the same time, every Monday, Wednesday, Friday and Saturday. Once she got past the first 21 days, she discovered that regular exercise felt good and she didn't want to stop. In essence, creating a habit leveraged her motivation.

Stephanie decided to evaluate her plan and her progress once a week. She also used these evaluations to periodically take a photo of herself. She then posted these updated photos on her refrigerator and pantry so she could clearly see the progress she was making.

On the following pages are Stephanie's Checklist, Successability Blueprint and Motivation Map. Together they represent her customized motivation plan for achieving her Vision.

Sample Self-Motivation Plans

STEPHANIE'S MOTIVATION PLAN CHECKLIST FOR BEING SLIM

Strategies to maximize the motivational power of the Vision:

- ✓ Focus on the "whys"
- ❑ Do a cost analysis
- ✓ Replace rather than eliminate
- ✓ Write your Vision as an affirmation and visualize it every day

Strategies to increase your Successability:

- ✓ Know your strengths
- ❑ Examine your self-imposed limitations and self-fulfilling prophecies
- ❑ Discover your stories of achievement
- ✓ Focus on what you can control
- ❑ Enhance your abilities
- ❑ Create success experiences
- ✓ **Divide and Conquer super strategy – create your own unique Successability Blueprint**

Strategies to maximize the motivational impact of your *Physical Environment*:

- ❑ Set up your Physical Environment so that you can be productive
- ✓ Set up your Physical Environment so that it is inspiring
- ✓ Minimize distractions
- ✓ Use "vision reminders"

Strategies to maximize the motivational impact of your *Social Environment*:

- ✓ Enlist positive family and friends in your journey

- ✓ Find a peer partner
- ✓ Join a support group
- ❏ Find a mentor

Strategies for overcoming detractors:
- ❏ Turn naysayers and their negativity into a positive motivational force by seeing the situation as a challenge
- ✓ Become your #1 cheerleader by constantly using positive self-talk
- ❏ Remember past courageous acts and leverage the courage you already have
- ❏ Eliminate excuses by asking, "If I couldn't use that excuse, what would I do differently?"
- ❏ Use a visual or kinesthetic reminder to catch and stop yourself when you complain
- ❏ Train yourself to increase your frustration tolerance
- ✓ Capitalize on perceived failures by seeing each as an unwanted result and an opportunity for learning

Strategies for dealing with distractions:
- ✓ Eliminate or minimize the distraction
- ✓ Turn your distractions into motivators
- ❏ Set boundaries or parameters for distractions that can't/shouldn't be avoided

Strategies for enhancing your motivation:
- ✓ Revisit your vision
- ✓ Leverage your motivation
- ✓ Develop good habits
- ❏ Make a promise
- ❏ Be open to inspiration and opportunities
- ❏ Identify your unique motivators

STEPHANIE'S SUCCESSABILITY BLUEPRINT FOR BEING SLIM

VISION: ME SLIM
(which means lose the weight *and* keep it off)

GOAL: Lose 35 pounds – start date May 30
Task: Join Weight Watchers – June 3
- ✦ Find the three closest locations – May 30
- ✦ Attend meetings at each location – June 1-10
- ✦ Decide which meeting times work best with my schedule – June 2
- ✦ Choose and join the group I am most comfortable with and has the best times for my schedule – June 12

Task: Set date to achieve goal of losing 35 pounds – June 15
Task: Go to meetings – ongoing
Task: Follow the program – ongoing
Task: Make a friend in Weight Watchers – June 17

GOAL: Develop healthy eating habits – start date June 5
Task: Define healthy eating habits – June 7
Task: Eat junk food only one day a week – ongoing
- ✦ Determine which day I will eat junk food – June 7
- ✦ Define "junk food" so I'm sure I won't eat it the other days – June 7
- ✦ Make sure there is no junk food in my house except on junk food day, so I'm not tempted to blow my plan on non-junk food days – ongoing

Task: Keep healthy foods handy so I always have healthy foods to eat – ongoing
- ✦ Determine what healthy foods I like – June 10
- ✦ Buy the "healthy foods" – ongoing
- ✦ Clean and prep any vegetables that need it so they are readily accessible to me – ongoing

GOAL: Exercise regularly – start date June 10
Task: Join a gym – June 30
- Make a list of four gyms to visit – June 15
    Find gyms that are conveniently located – June 10
    Talk to friends for recommendations – June 10-15
- Visit all four gyms (do NOT feel pressured to join until all visits are made) – June 15-30
- Pick the gym I want to join and make the best deal – June 30

Task: Decide what type of exercise I want to do – July 15
- Make a list of exercises that seem fun – June 10
- Find out where I can try them out – June 12
- Try them out – June 15-July 15
- Decide which one I like best and fits my needs – July 15

Task: Hire a trainer – July 25
- Discuss with gym staff my needs and which trainer would be best for me – July 15
- Interview three trainers – July 16-25
- Pick the one I like the best – July 25

Task: Get a walking partner (maybe my Weight Watchers friend?) – June 24

Task: Track my exercise with an exercise log – ongoing
- Buy an exercise log that fits my needs – June 20

GOAL: Set up a system of rewards for success – start date June 15
Task: Determine what rewards I would like and would motivate me – June 18
Task: Set criteria for earning rewards – June 20

Sample Self-Motivation Plans

Stephanie's Motivation Map

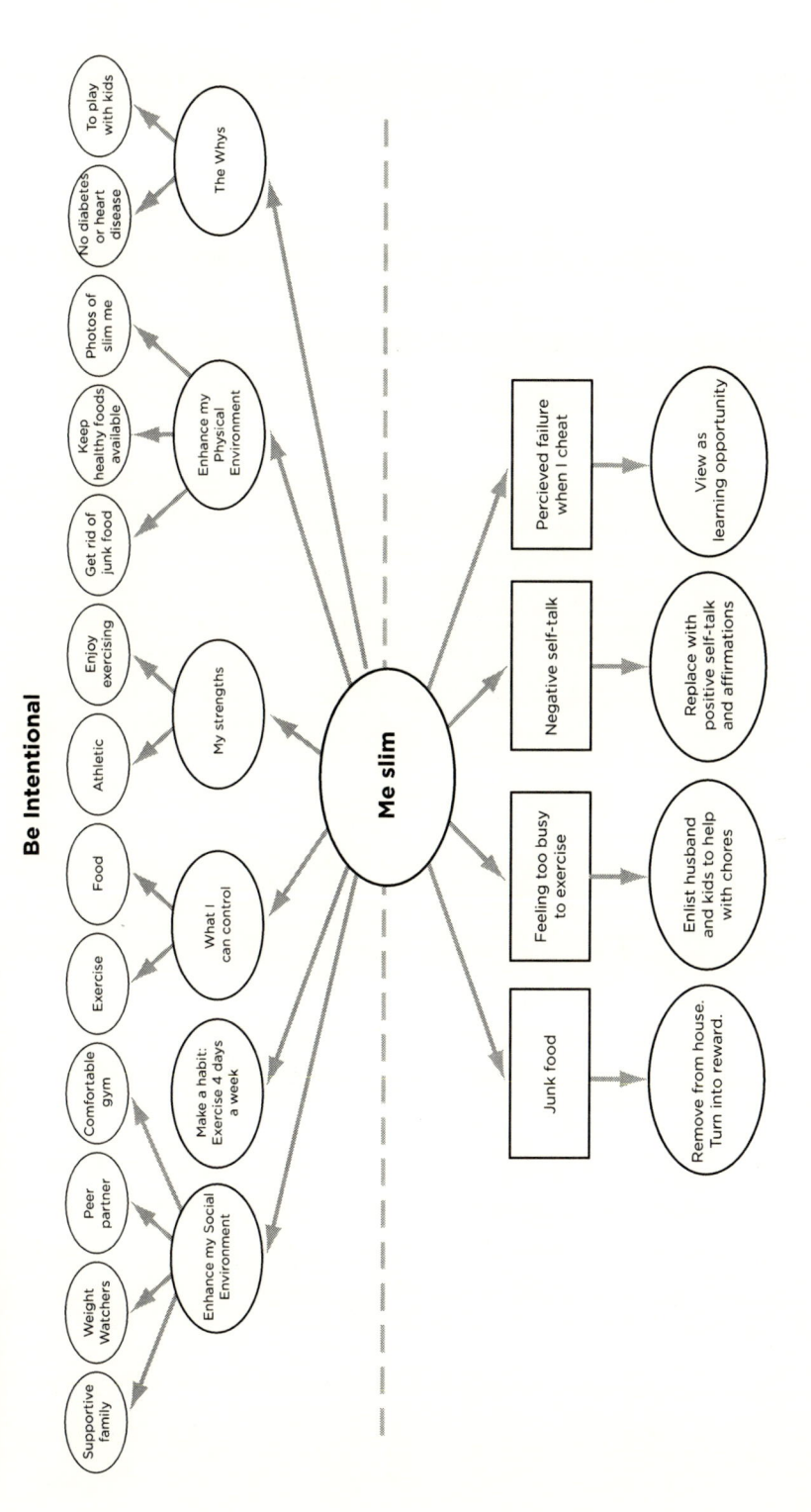

Be Intentional

Me slim

The Whys:
- To play with kids
- No diabetes or heart disease

Enhance my Physical Environment:
- Photos of slim me
- Keep healthy foods available
- Get rid of junk food

My strengths:
- Enjoy exercising
- Athletic

What I can control:
- Food
- Exercise

Make a habit: Exercise 4 days a week

Enhance my Social Environment:
- Comfortable gym
- Peer partner
- Weight Watchers
- Supportive family

Perceived failure when I cheat → View as learning opportunity

Negative self-talk → Replace with positive self-talk and affirmations

Feeling too busy to exercise → Enlist husband and kids to help with chores

Junk food → Remove from house. Turn into reward.

153

Career/Job Change

One common change many people want in their lives has to do with their career or profession. This is an extremely stressful change; in fact, a job change is one of the top stressors, after only a death in the family and a divorce. It is no wonder that so many of us are hesitant to seek a better job, even if we are unhappy in our present one.

I am frequently asked whether one can use the VSE Model for Self-Motivation to find a job. The answer is that the VSE model can be used for any change you want to make in your life, even a change involving your job, whether you are unemployed and looking for a new job or currently employed and looking for a different job. If you have been dreaming about getting a job, finding a better job, changing careers or even starting your own business, creating a customized motivation plan can help you make your dream come true.

When one is unemployed, there is a certain inherent motivation for finding a job – you need to keep a roof over your head and put food on the table! However, it can be difficult to stay motivated if you are discouraged. In poor economic times, many unemployed people give up looking for a job because they lack confidence that they will be successful in their search. Without confidence, they are not motivated to even try.

For those who are employed but seek something better, it can be equally difficult to get and stay motivated. Often, it isn't so much that they don't like their job, but more that they feel stuck in a rut. Yet that rut is familiar and oddly comfortable, and they rationalize that at least they have a job that pays the bills. From a motivation standpoint, this is a bad place to be. When people are miserable in their job, they tend to be more motivated to seek something new.

It's when the situation is tolerable that inertia takes over, and it's all too easy to stay stuck in the rut.

Let's see how one might apply the Self-Motivation Model to finding a job, no matter the circumstances.

Chris had been employed for the last five years as a contract negotiator, and she was very good at what she did. But over time, she became dissatisfied with her job. It was unfulfilling and, quite frankly, boring. She'd negotiated all the contracts in her portfolio twice, and work was no longer a challenge professionally. She got along okay with her boss, and the company she worked for was just average in terms of culture and employee relations. She didn't dislike her job, but she couldn't say that she liked it, either. It was time for a change.

Because she had a job and wasn't miserable in it, Chris knew that the very first step was to determine just how worthwhile this Vision was. She wondered if moving to another job or company would just mean more of the same. Perhaps the grass only looks greener on the other side … until you actually get over there and see all the dead brown patches. She spent a few days pondering two questions:

Why is finding a new job important to me?

What exactly do I want in a new job?

After much thought, she came to some exciting conclusions. She wrote her Vision, "Find a purposeful and rewarding job in a non-profit organization," on a note card. Below her Vision she wrote down her answers to the two questions and posted the note card on her closet door where she would see it at least twice every day – when she got ready for work in the morning and again when she changed clothes after work. That was when she really needed a motivation boost — at the end of a long day when she just wanted to relax, eat dinner and curl up with a good book.

Chris was a successful, confident professional. She realized, however, that because her Vision involved finding a job in a different profession and even a different type of organization, she would be wise to utilize some Successability strategies. First, she made a list of her strengths that would be particularly helpful for non-profit and charitable organizations. Chris then committed to focusing on only those things she had control over. Ultimately, she couldn't control whether she got a particular job. But she had total control over her behaviors and actions, such as networking, improving her skills, preparing for interviews and ensuring her image and appearance were professional.

Because her past experience would not be as helpful or pertinent to her new profession, Chris knew she had to enhance her skills. She signed up for a leadership seminar her company offered, registered for some business classes at a local college and researched non-profit administration on the web.

Chris came to the conclusion that one of the best ways for her to get exposure in this new profession was to do some networking. But she hadn't done much networking in the past; so this was one area where she felt less confident and somewhat uncomfortable. So she developed a plan to take small steps and create success experiences. She decided she would go to the first networking opportunity only to observe. Once she successfully accomplished that, she set a goal to introduce herself to one person at the next event and to two people at the event after that. Within a few months, Chris was a networking guru. She discovered that when she genuinely focused on other people and helped them make connections, they naturally wanted to help her in return.

To maximize the motivational impact of her Physical Environment, Chris spent an entire Saturday cleaning up and organizing her home office. Over time, she had accumulated stacks of bills, tax documents and papers that needed to be filed. Her desk was covered with photographs and supplies for a scrapbook she was making. This was definitely not a space that was conducive to launching an effective job search. But by the end of the weekend, she had created an Environment dedicated to pursuing her Vision.

Chris's parents, brothers and boyfriend were very supportive of her desire to change careers, and she appreciated their positive attitude. But none of them had any experience in the non-profit world, and she was learning that it was quite different than the corporate world. She needed to find a mentor who could counsel and guide her. Then she remembered that she'd met the director of a local shelter for abused women and children at a fundraising event several months ago. She contacted the woman and asked if she would be willing to mentor her, and they had their first meeting the following week.

Not married and not one to watch much TV, Chris didn't have many distractions – except, that is, for her boyfriend. But he was a good kind of distraction. Of course, their prime time together was nights and weekends when they were both off work – precisely the same time she needed to be working on her Vision. Together they decided that she would pursue her Vision for an hour and a half three nights a week and Saturday mornings, while he went to the gym to work out, something he hadn't done much of since they started dating. Realizing they were each other's biggest distraction, setting a schedule helped both of them manifest their Visions and yet still left plenty of time to be together.

Over the following months, Chris interviewed for several positions, but she never received a call for a second interview or a job offer.

Frustrated, she contacted her mentor, who suggested she view the situation as a learning opportunity and advised her on next steps. Chris called the interviewers and asked for feedback. She quickly learned that although each interviewer had liked her skill set and attitude, she was at a distinct disadvantage compared to the other candidates because she had no prior non-profit experience. At her mentor's suggestion, she began volunteering on the weekends at various agencies and shelters to better learn the ins and outs of non-profit organizations.

Although it took her nearly a year to achieve her Vision, Chris found it was well worth the time and effort. Her new non-profit job is fulfilling and meaningful, and she wakes up every day excited about going to work. On the following pages are the Checklist and Motivation Map that helped Chris manifest her Vision.

Sample Self-Motivation Plans

Chris's Motivation Plan Checklist for Career Change

Strategies to maximize the motivational power of the Vision:

- ✓ Focus on the "whys"
- ❏ Do a cost analysis
- ❏ Replace rather than eliminate
- ❏ Write your Vision as an affirmation and visualize it every day

Strategies to increase your Successability:

- ✓ Know your strengths
- ❏ Examine your self-imposed limitations and self-fulfilling prophecies
- ❏ Discover your stories of achievement
- ✓ Focus on what you can control
- ✓ Enhance your abilities
- ✓ Create success experiences
- ❏ **Divide and Conquer super strategy – create your own unique Successability Blueprint**

Strategies to maximize the motivational impact of your *Physical Environment*:

- ✓ Set up your Physical Environment so that you can be productive
- ❏ Set up your Physical Environment so that it is inspiring
- ❏ Minimize distractions
- ✓ Use "vision reminders"

Strategies to maximize the motivational impact of your *Social Environment*:

- ✓ Enlist positive family and friends in your journey

- ❏ Find a peer partner
- ❏ Join a support group
- ✓ Find a mentor

Strategies for overcoming detractors:

- ❏ Turn naysayers and their negativity into a positive motivational force by seeing the situation as a challenge
- ❏ Become your #1 cheerleader by constantly using positive self-talk
- ❏ Remember past courageous acts and leverage the courage you already have
- ❏ Eliminate excuses by asking, "If I couldn't use that excuse, what would I do differently?"
- ❏ Use a visual or kinesthetic reminder to catch and stop yourself when you complain
- ❏ Train yourself to increase your frustration tolerance
- ✓ Capitalize on perceived failures by seeing each as an unwanted result and an opportunity for learning

Strategies for dealing with distractions:

- ❏ Eliminate or minimize the distraction
- ❏ Turn your distractions into motivators
- ✓ Set boundaries or parameters for distractions that can't/shouldn't be avoided

Strategies for enhancing your motivation:

- ❏ Revisit your vision
- ❏ Leverage your motivation
- ❏ Develop good habits
- ❏ Make a promise
- ✓ Be open to inspiration and opportunities
- ❏ Identify your unique motivators

Sample Self-Motivation Plans

Chris's Motivation Map

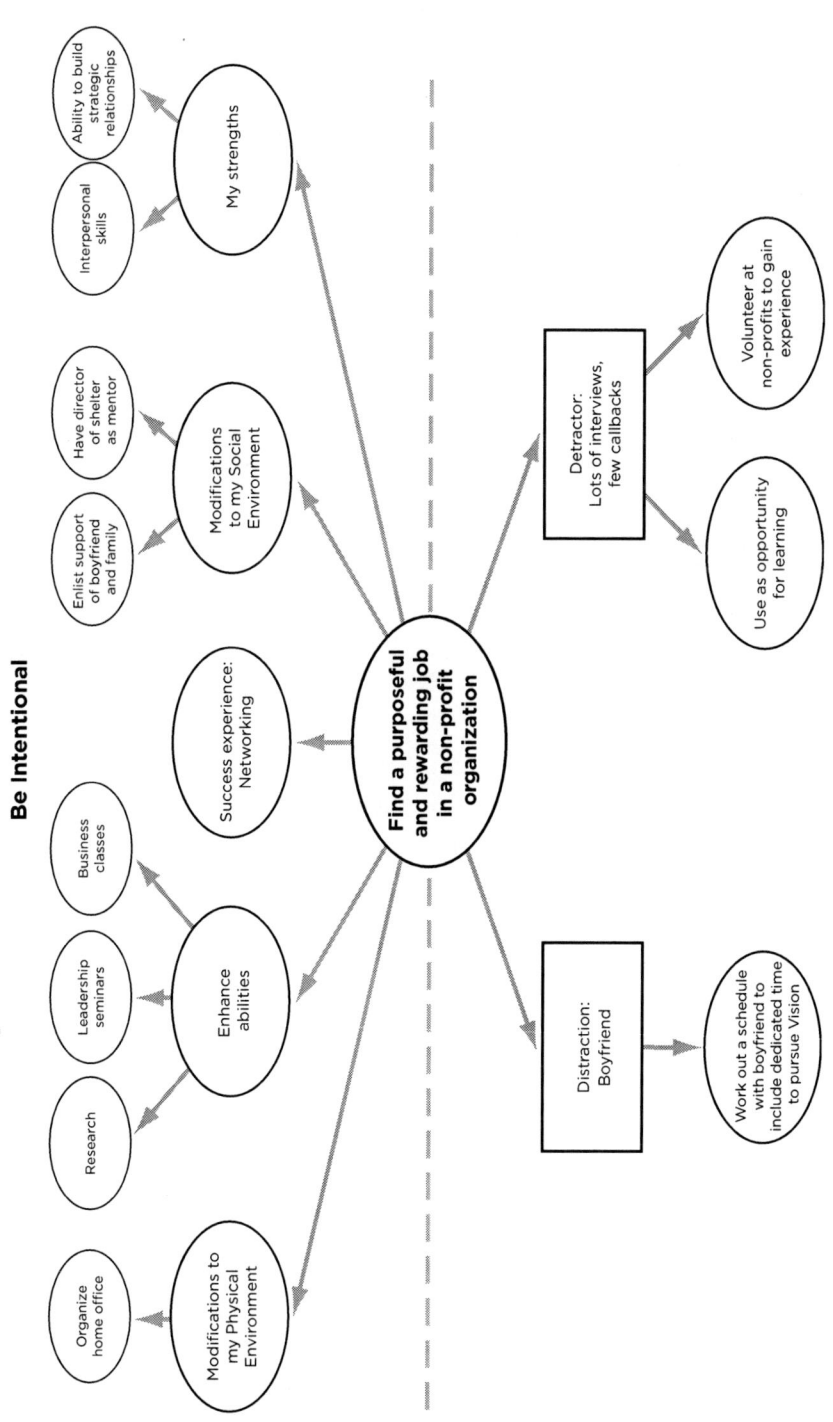

Be Intentional

- **Find a purposeful and rewarding job in a non-profit organization** (central goal)

- **My strengths**
  - Ability to build strategic relationships
  - Interpersonal skills

- **Modifications to my Social Environment**
  - Have director of shelter as mentor
  - Enlist support of boyfriend and family

- **Success experience: Networking**

- **Enhance abilities**
  - Business classes
  - Leadership seminars
  - Research

- **Modifications to my Physical Environment**
  - Organize home office

- **Detractor: Lots of interviews, few callbacks**
  - Volunteer at non-profits to gain experience
  - Use as opportunity for learning

- **Distraction: Boyfriend**
  - Work out a schedule with boyfriend to include dedicated time to pursue Vision

161

Finances

I find financial matters to be of special interest because they affect almost all of us, especially in tough economic times. Too many people are becoming mired in more and more debt. Many of them feel as if their "life blood is being sucked away" and want a path toward financial freedom, a place where they control their finances rather than their finances controlling them. Furthermore, financial troubles cause many domestic problems (even more than sex!), which is not surprising since so many of us have emotional baggage when it comes to money. So let's see how one intentional man – I'll refer to him as Rod – applied the VSE Model for Self-Motivation to his finances.

Rod was living paycheck to paycheck, had no savings and had significant credit-card debt that was creeping ever higher. He hadn't hit bottom by any means – he was employed and able to pay the minimum due on his credit cards every month with enough left over to pay his bills – but he could see the writing on the wall and it wasn't black. He knew he had to make some major changes, but he just couldn't get motivated. He wasn't able to say no to his wants, be it the newest video game or going out drinking with his friends. Month after month, his credit-card debt grew, and it was taking more of his income to pay the minimum. Then he found out about the Model for Self-Motivation and decided to create his own motivation plan.

For his Vision, Rod decided on "Me as a fiscally responsible adult," a positive affirmation. He liked that the Vision wasn't only about eliminating debt or building a savings account, but instead addressed a fundamental change, from him as an irresponsible child who always satisfied himself to the responsible grownup he always knew, deep inside, he was.

Rod was quite clear on the reasons why he wanted to gain control of his finances, but to burn the value of this change into his mind, he wrote them down, knowing that the process of getting them on paper would provide further clarity. He wrote down: *reduced stress, ability to buy things I need (rather than want), down payment for new car or house, money for retirement* and *a feeling of pride at how responsible I am.*

Yet he thought these weren't enough to keep him motivated. So he also focused on the cost of *not* taking action, on what would happen if he failed to change his financial ways: maxing out his credit cards, falling behind on payments, not being creditworthy, possibly losing his car and perhaps even having to file bankruptcy.

Rod was a big believer in the power of visualization, so every morning and evening he spent five minutes envisioning what his life would be like when he achieved his Vision. He saw himself living within his means and felt the satisfaction that would bring. He thought about making the final payment on each credit card and seeing the zero balance on the statement. And he visualized himself opening an investment account and eagerly watching it grow.

For the second factor, Successability, Rod used my favorite strategy: Divide and Conquer. He created a Successability Blueprint, a clear plan for how he would make this financial change happen. He wrote down all the steps he could think of and came to the exciting realization that when he had accomplished his goals, he would be well on his way to being the fiscally responsible adult he wanted to be. Through the process of creating his Blueprint, he also gained clarity about what regaining control of his finances actually meant to him and how he would know when he had achieved it.

Rod decided that a key part of his plan was to increase his financial intelligence. First, he went to www.usa.gov and typed "debt relief" into the search screen. There he found a wealth of information and assistance. He also thought about credit counseling as a resource, but knew he needed to find a reputable company. He checked out the Federal Trade Commission's website (http://www.ftc.gov/bcp/edu/pubs/consumer/credit/cre13.shtm) and researched various credit counseling companies. Eventually, he found one he was comfortable with, and a counselor there taught him how to make and follow a budget. He also recognized that his credit counselor was more or less a mentor when it came to financial issues.

His final Successability strategy was to create a success experience. He set a challenge for himself – to pay off one credit card – and committed to it. When he accomplished that several months later, he knew he could pay off the rest. He also started a small investment account, funding it with a small payroll deduction from every pay check.

When he looked at his Environment, Rod saw how his Social Environment, namely his drinking buddies, had played a large part in his lack of motivation to change his fiscal irresponsibility. He quickly realized he would need to change his Social Environment so that it positively, rather than negatively, impacted his motivation. He knew he had to make a choice: either convert one or more of his drinking buddies to non-drinking buddies – maybe even making one of them a peer partner in his mission – or get new friends. This was a gut check for Rod: it's not always easy to make changes.

To increase the motivational power of his Physical Environment, Rod made a copy of each credit-card statement. He used "white out" to remove the current balances, replaced them with "$0" and wrote "PAID IN FULL" in red ink across each one. Then he posted them around his home – on the refrigerator, on his bathroom mirror and by his computer. Whenever he got discouraged, he looked at those statements and thought about how incredible it would feel when they were actually paid off.

Knowing that buying the latest video game was one of his detractors, Rod cancelled his subscription to a gaming magazine. If he didn't know about the new releases, he wouldn't be as tempted to go out and buy them. He also decided that he could rent new games for about $10 rather than buying them for $60 each (he found he was bored with them after a week anyway). That would save him $50!

Remembering something he'd heard Suze Orman say in *The 9 Steps to Financial Freedom* – "True financial freedom is not only having money, but having power over that money as well" – Rod made a conscious decision and promised himself that he would be in charge and in control of his financial life. He was the boss from now on!

But as Rod began his journey, he found that he became quite frustrated when he wanted to buy or do something he knew he shouldn't. One such evening when his buddies called him to go out with them and he was on the verge of giving in, he remembered the strategy about increasing frustration tolerance. Instead of getting dressed to go out, he grabbed a beer, sat down in his overstuffed chair and just experienced the frustration. Then he told himself, "I would much rather go out with my friends, but if I don't, it won't kill me. I can live with this." And he did, in fact, survive the evening without going out. Rod was able to internalize the reality that frustration may be uncomfortable and inconvenient, but that it is a part of life that he could live with.

Finally, Rod knew there was a very unique motivator that would help him stay on track to achieve his Vision. He'd wanted to go on a photo safari to Africa for quite some time, ever since hearing friends talk about their vacation experience. He promised himself that when all his credit cards were paid off and he had saved the money for the trip, he would take it. He got a travel brochure about Africa and kept it in his car. When he was tempted to stop at the video game store or go out drinking with his buddies, he'd sit in his car and look at that brochure.

Given the monthly nature of budgeting and credit-card statements, Rod decided to evaluate his motivation plan once a month. On the following pages are his Checklist, Successability Blueprint and Motivation Map. Together they represent his customized motivation plan for achieving financial freedom.

Rod's Motivation Plan Checklist for Financial Change

Strategies to maximize the motivational power of the Vision:

- ✓ Focus on the "whys"
- ✓ Do a cost analysis
- ✓ Replace rather than eliminate
- ✓ Write your Vision as an affirmation and visualize it every day

Strategies to increase your Successability:

- ❏ Know your strengths
- ❏ Examine your self-imposed limitations and self-fulfilling prophecies
- ❏ Discover your stories of achievement
- ❏ Focus on what you can control
- ✓ Enhance your abilities
- ✓ Create success experiences
- ✓ **Divide and Conquer super strategy – create your own unique Successability Blueprint**

Strategies to maximize the motivational impact of your *Physical Environment*:

- ❏ Set up your Physical Environment so that you can be productive
- ✓ Set up your Physical Environment so that it is inspiring
- ✓ Minimize distractions
- ✓ Use "vision reminders"

Strategies to maximize the motivational impact of your *Social Environment*:

- ❏ Enlist positive family and friends in your journey

✓ Find a peer partner
❏ Join a support group
✓ Find a mentor

Strategies for overcoming detractors:

❏ Turn naysayers and their negativity into a positive motivational force by seeing the situation as a challenge

❏ Become your #1 cheerleader by constantly using positive self-talk

❏ Remember past courageous acts and leverage the courage you already have

❏ Eliminate excuses by asking, "If I couldn't use that excuse, what would I do differently?"

❏ Use a visual or kinesthetic reminder to catch and stop yourself when you complain

✓ Train yourself to increase your frustration tolerance

❏ Capitalize on perceived failures by seeing each as an unwanted result and an opportunity for learning

Strategies for dealing with distractions:

✓ Eliminate or minimize the distraction

❏ Turn your distractions into motivators

❏ Set boundaries or parameters for distractions that can't/shouldn't be avoided

Strategies for enhancing your motivation:

❏ Revisit your vision
❏ Leverage your motivation
❏ Develop good habits
✓ Make a promise
❏ Be open to inspiration and opportunities
✓ Identify your unique motivators

Rod's Successability Blueprint for Financial Change

Vision: Me as a Fiscally Responsible Adult

Goal: Live within a budget
Task: Find out how to make a budget
- ✦ Search web for information on budgeting
- ✦ Read the information

Task: Create the budget
- ✦ Go to a credit counselor for assistance on how to make a budget

Task: Live within the budget
- ✦ Track spending for a certain period of time

Task: Revise the budget as needed

Goal: Make fiscally responsible decisions and choices
Task: Don't carry credit cards with me
Task: Before I make any non-essential purchases over $20, delay the purchase for two days and review to see if I still want the item.

Goal: Pay off credit cards
Task: Stop using credit cards – cut them up
Task: Work with credit counselor to create payment plan with creditors
Task: Set aside a set percent of each regular paycheck to use toward paying off debt
Task: Get a part-time job for a while to catch up on debt

Goal: Have an investment account
Task: Determine how much I can afford to save
Task: Contact employer for information on payroll deduction for automatic savings
Task: Start payroll deduction

Rod's Motivation Map

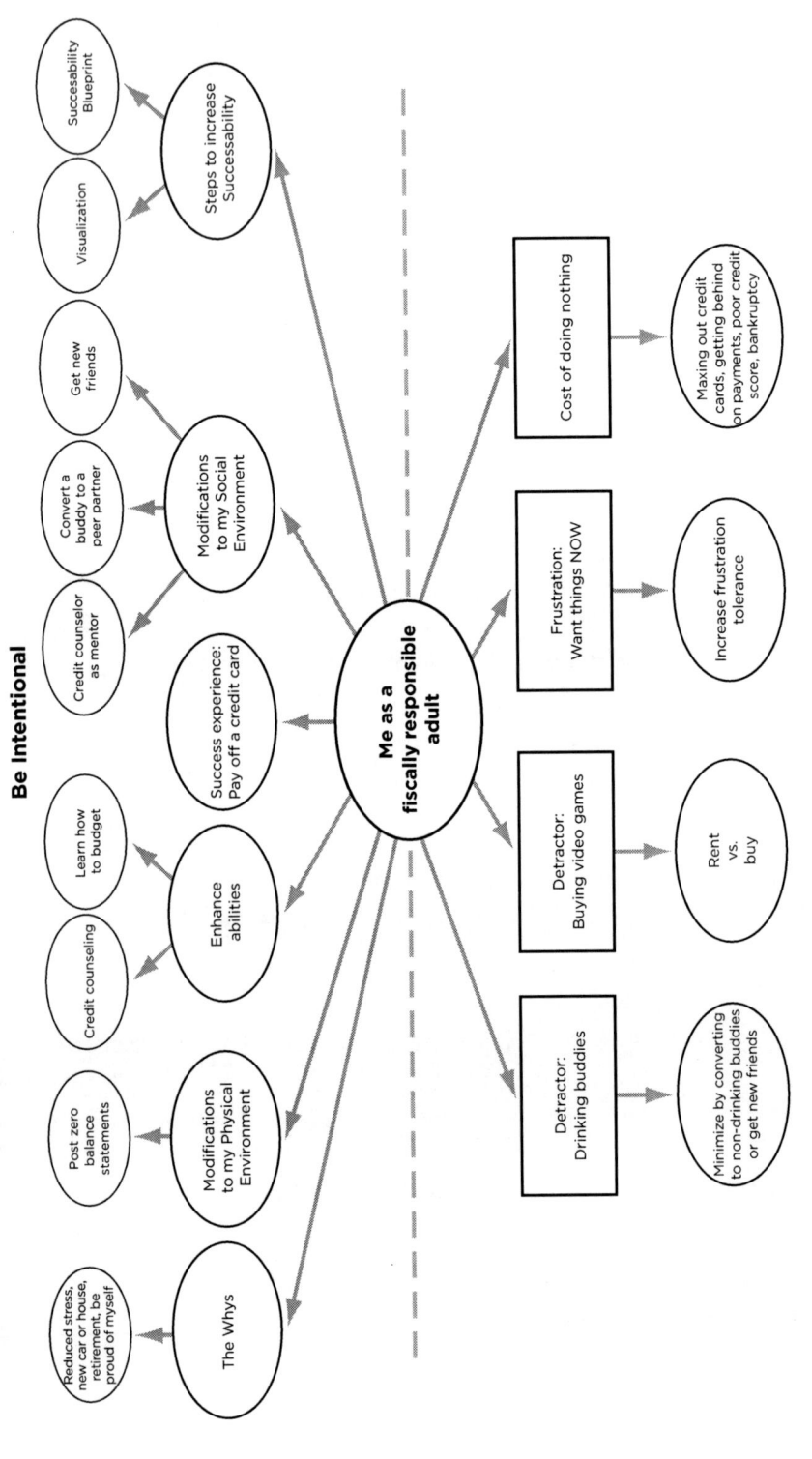

Be Intentional

Me as a fiscally responsible adult

Steps to increase Successability
- Successability Blueprint
- Visualization

Modifications to my Social Environment
- Get new friends
- Convert a buddy to a peer partner
- Credit counselor as mentor

Success experience: Pay off a credit card

Enhance abilities
- Learn how to budget
- Credit counseling

Modifications to my Physical Environment
- Post zero balance statements

The Whys
- Reduced stress, new car or house, retirement, be proud of myself

Cost of doing nothing → Maxing out credit cards, getting behind on payments, poor credit score, bankruptcy

Frustration: Want things NOW → Increase frustration tolerance

Detractor: Buying video games → Rent vs. buy

Detractor: Drinking buddies → Minimize by converting to non-drinking buddies or get new friends

*"You can motivate by fear.
And you can motivate by reward.
But both of those methods are only temporary.
The only lasting thing is self-motivation."*

– HOMER RICE

iMotivateme

Index

ability	5, 7, 9, 10, 12, 29, 30, 34, 35, 38, 41, 42, 64, 80, 86, 94, 103, 117, 163
automatic	9, 10, 11, 87, 106
automatic mode	64, 90, 95
Bandura, Albert	30, 40, 41
blame game	91, 92, 98
bridge the Gap	134, 135, 139
Christian, Kenneth	45, 97
clarity	16, 17, 31, 32, 35, 41-44, 48, 50, 52, 54, 85, 122, 133, 146, 163
commitment	18, 25, 26, 50, 106, 108, 143
control	9-12, 24, 30, 31, 36, 37, 41-45, 48, 52, 54, 55, 64, 76, 82, 85, 92, 120, 125, 132, 146, 156, 162, 163, 165
cost analysis	21, 27, 120
courage	84-86, 98, 121, 130, 132, 133
Deci, Edward L.	30
detractor	76, 79, 80, 86, 95, 97, 99, 101, 102, 121, 126, 127, 136, 165
distractions	10, 48, 67-69, 76, 86, 87-91, 98, 105, 107, 109, 112, 120, 121, 126, 134, 136, 147, 149, 150, 157, 159
Divide and Conquer	43-46, 49, 53, 54, 56, 106, 120, 122, 145, 163
Drucker ratio	132, 137, 139
education	6, 39, 81
environment	6-8, 12, 36, 39, 63-71, 74-76, 80-82, 90, 102, 108, 111, 120, 125-127, 135, 136, 143, 146, 157, 164
evaluation	129-139
fear	55, 80, 83-86, 98, 126, 171
feeling of having failed	95, 98
Frankl, Viktor	9, 10
frustration	93-95, 98, 121, 127, 165, 168
frustration tolerance/ tolerance for frustration	94, 98, 121, 165
Gap	133-137, 139
goal	4, 5, 8, 9, 11, 30, 35, 44-54, 57-60, 68, 71, 80, 86, 89, 95, 98, 102, 106, 111, 122, 133-136, 139, 145-147, 151, 152, 156, 163, 169
Goethe	26
How Not to Be Afraid of Your Own Life	84
identify the Gap	133
intention	9, 10, 12, 13, 15, 34, 64
intentional man/woman/person	35, 55, 64, 96, 162
Keller, John	5
leveraging motivation	65, 84-86, 98, 103-106, 108, 112, 121, 148

Man's Search for Meaning	9
mentor	39, 70, 71, 74-76, 107, 109, 112, 121, 126, 157, 158, 164
Motivation Map/ Motivation Mapping	4, 118, 122, 123-128, 133, 134, 137, 143, 148, 153, 158, 161, 166, 170
Motivation Plan	4, 19, 59, 117, 118, 120, 122, 123, 127-130, 136, 137, 139, 142, 143, 145, 146, 148, 149, 154, 159, 162, 166, 167
Motivation Plan Checklist	120, 149, 159, 167
naysayers	80-83, 97, 121, 126
peer partner	70, 72-76, 106, 107, 109, 112, 120, 126, 147, 164
Physical Environment	7, 63-70, 76, 81, 90, 102, 111, 120, 126, 127, 146, 157, 164
Piver, Susan	84
Redmoon, Ambrose Hollingsworth	84
resources	4, 8, 25, 33, 39, 66, 74, 143, 164
revisit your vision	102, 112, 121
risk	39, 84, 85, 95, 98, 131
role model	70
self-imposed limitations	33, 34, 42, 120, 126
self-praise	132, 137, 139
Social Environment	7, 8, 63, 64, 67, 70, 71, 74-76, 80, 92, 108, 120, 143, 146, 164, 167
stories of achievement	35, 36, 42, 55, 83, 120, 125
Successability	7, 8, 12, 29-33, 35, 40-45, 47-49, 47-49, 51-57, 59, 61, 122, 125, 127, 128, 133-137, 143, 145, 146, 148, 151, 156, 163, 164, 166, 169
Successability Blueprint	44, 45, 49, 51-57, 59-61, 65, 84, 118, 120, 122, 127, 128, 133, 134, 136, 137, 143, 145, 148, 151, 163, 166, 169
support group	9, 70, 72-76, 97, 121, 126, 146
Tarkenton, Fran	130
task	4, 10, 30, 44-54, 57-60, 86, 89, 94, 98, 102-107, 112, 127, 133-135, 139, 145, 151, 152, 169
The Psychology of Self-Determination	30
training opportunities	126
valuing the vision	19
Vision	7, 12-27, 29-57, 59-61, 63-69, 71-76, 79-81, 83-90, 93-98
vision reminders	68, 69, 76, 93
VSE Self-Motivation Model/ Self-Motivation Model	6, 9, 13, 79, 155
worthwhile pursuit	14, 16-18, 24, 63, 81, 127
Your Own Worst Enemy: Breaking the Habit of Adult Underachievement	45, 97

About the Author

Bob Prentiss, JD, MS, DTM, is an expert on the science of self-motivation. Known as the Non-Motivational Speaker™, he is a teacher of self-motivation rather than a motivator. His mission is to show others how to motivate themselves 24/7 in order to achieve their dreams and goals.

An engaging writer and dynamic speaker, Bob is frequently sought after for his interactive presentations and innate ability to quickly connect with audiences of all sizes and compositions. His extensive experience in instructional design enables him to fully customize his presentations for groups and organizations for maximum results. Bob has achieved the designation of Distinguished Toastmaster, the highest designation awarded by Toastmasters International.

Currently, Bob is assistant general counsel for the Florida Office of Insurance Regulation, where he is in charge of rulemaking for the agency. In addition, he analyzes and drafts legislation and advises regulators on matters involving licensure and regulatory actions against licensees. He also serves as an expert witness for the federal government in their criminal prosecutions of viatical fraud, a particularly heinous form of insurance fraud.

Bob received his Bachelor's degree from U.C. Berkeley, his law degree from the University of San Francisco and a Master's of Instructional Design from Florida State University.

Bob is the proud father of two grown children, Jeremey and Beth. He currently serves on the Board of Directors for Ability 1st, North Florida's Center for Independent Living, and continues to be a very active member of Toastmasters.

FREE Resources to Help You Get and Stay Motivated

Take your motivation to the next level and achieve your goals and dreams with these essential *iMOTIVATEme* resources:

- ❖ *iMOTIVATEme* **Blog** – regular, ongoing support and insights to help you achieve your Vision. FREE subscription at www.bobaprentiss.com/blog.

- ❖ **Social Media** – connect with Bob and other people just like you who are working toward their goals and dreams. Follow Bob on Twitter @BobPrentiss.

- ❖ *iMOTIVATEme* **Workbook** – an all-inclusive resource where you can complete the iMotivate exercises. FREE download from www.iMotivateMeTheBook.com.

- ❖ **VSE™ Self-Motivation Model** – a full-color version of the Self-Motivation Model that will remind you to stay intentional and enhance your motivation. FREE download from www.iMotivateMeTheBook.com.

- ❖ **Motivation Plan Checklist** – a comprehensive list of self-motivation strategies to help you maximize the impact of your individualized Motivation Plan. FREE download from www.iMotivateMeTheBook.com.

- ❖ **Motivation Map Template** – a handy template to help you easily create a visual representation of your customized Motivation Plan. Post your completed map in your Physical Environment and watch your motivation soar. FREE download from www.iMotivateMeTheBook.com.

- ❖ **Motivation Plan Evaluation Guide** – an easy-to-follow outline that will make your self-evaluations effective and efficient. FREE download from www.iMotivateMeTheBook.com.

For additional resources to enhance your self-motivation so you can achieve all your goals and dreams, visit www.iMotivateMeTheBook.com or www.BobAPrentiss.com.

Bring the Power of Self-Motivation to Your Organization

Invite author **Bob Prentiss, The Non-Motivational Speaker**™, to bring the power of self-motivation to your group. Bob understands that lasting motivation is an internal rather than an external issue, and that's why the impact of traditional motivational speakers wears off quickly. Bob is passionate about teaching the science and art of self-motivation in order to create positive, long-term habit change. When people learn to motivate themselves, they are able to:

- Stay focused,
- Take consistent action,
- Ignore distractions,
- Minimize frustration in the midst of challenges,
- Make their goals and dreams a reality.

With a delightful and engaging style, Bob shares proven self-motivational strategies through humor and real-life examples participants can easily relate to. *iMOTIVATEme* presentations give participants the skills they need to take charge of their own motivation in order to achieve their professional, personal, lifestyle and financial goals. Participants will:

- Learn the proprietary VSE™ Model for Self-Motivation;
- Determine their unique motivators and de-motivators;
- Identify specific strategies they can put to use immediately to increase their motivation;
- Create their own customized Motivation Plan;
- Walk away with tools and resources to keep their motivation high.

iMOTIVATEme presentations are ideal for businesses, associations, churches and non-profits, and can be customized to meet your organization's specific objectives and conference themes. Formats range from one-hour keynotes to powerful breakout sessions and full-day interactive workshops.

To book Bob for your next meeting or conference, visit www.BobAPrentiss.com or email speaking@BobAPrentiss.com.

iMotivate
me

www.iMotivateMeTheBook.com

Retenoids — Prescription strength

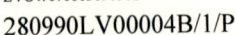

- Tretinoid
- Retinol — based cream, over the counter
- less than $20
- Best antiaging 2-3 times in evening
- up to every night

- sugar
- sat fat
- salt — I package processed foods
- C Processed meal in restaurants
- alternatives to salt
- antioxidants —
  - Cinnamon
  - Cumin
  - Oregano
  - Rosemary

Food should be (like the great lakes)

- sun blocks — wear sunglasses
- UBA — not UBB — skiing
- Broad spectrum